# Bruce Cole

# The ... ndbook

...roach combining
...other techniques
...uides to projects

**ED 12405**
ISBN 0-946535-80-9

SCHOTT

www.schott-music.com

Mainz · London · Berlin · Madrid · New York · Paris · Prague · Tokyo · Toronto
© 1996 SCH...

*For Maggie, Hannah, and thanks to Katy for help with the graphics*

The author and publisher would like to thank Peter Nickol and Paul Terry
for their invaluable assistance in preparing this project for publication.

British Library Cataloguing-in-Publication Data.
A catalogue record of this book is available from the British Library

ED 12405
ISBN 0 946535 80 9

Typeset by Musonix Typesetting
Cover design The Design Works
Printed in Germany · S&Co. 7711

# Contents

# Introduction

# A note for the teacher ...

Of all the component parts of the modern music curriculum, composition tends to be regarded as the most forbidding. The original idea for this book came from the type of home improvement and do-it-yourself manuals which in simple language combine 'tricks of the trade' and other techniques with step-by-step guides to projects.

The text is aimed at the pupil, and most of the exercises and projects can be undertaken by the pupil working directly from the book. However, the input of the teacher is important, and to this end the book makes a number of assumptions: that the teacher will fill in historical background and listening material, and will, when necessary, play the musical examples to illustrate the text.

The earlier chapters are aimed at the beginner and involve a high proportion of group activities which will need help from a teacher. The chapters then move progressively towards independence, with the pupil encouraged to work alone or with a partner.

The following **plan of work** is intended to show the various topics as they are threaded through the chapters. It should be possible to use this plan to construct a project on a particular topic, such as ostinati, cadences or modulation, or perhaps to trace melody-writing from plainchant to rock. It also identifies exercises which would be suitable for groups of varying sizes.

## A plan of work

# ... and a note for the pupil

## Three good reasons for composing

England and Wales are two countries where composing music is a compulsory part of school study, as laid down in the National Curriculum.

A great many people find the idea of composing quite frightening. This is not surprising; until recently, the study of music consisted largely of listening, performing, and writing essays, but very rarely writing the music itself. Apart from exam exercises, composing was something only experts and advanced students did.

Then along came GCSE music, for which candidates have to start composing at the age of fourteen. After that came the National Curriculum, which requires pupils to be composing at seven. The age seems to be getting younger all the time, but the task gets no easier, either for you or your teacher.

So why should you compose? Here are three reasons:

▶ It can be enormously satisfying to fill the air with sounds you have made yourself, and to be able to share this expression with others.

▶ For many people, studying music consists of learning an instrument and playing music written by someone else. Composing involves you in the act of creation.

▶ Composing is a very useful way of finding out how music works. It teaches you music techniques from the inside. Even if you have no wish to become a composer, it will improve your playing and listening skills.

Whatever your reasons for composing, this book is intended as a do-it-yourself guide.

Parts I and II are aimed at the beginner. They start with activities organised by a teacher and intended for groups. These lead on to projects where you might work alone or with a friend to produce a piece.

Part III covers the study of harmony and counterpoint, which you may have to learn about for exams. Part IV introduces some of the techniques used in the music of this century. Part V covers popular music.

Like any textbook, *The Composer's Handbook* can be read and worked through from cover to cover or just dipped into. To help with this there is a list of contents at the front and an alphabetical index at the back. There is also, included in this introduction, a **plan of work**. This is a different type of index, in which similar topics are all grouped together. It should help you to trace ideas and techniques through the book.

*The Composer's Handbook* cannot take the place of a teacher, whose help you may need to play the written examples and provide ideas and advice. Nor will it provide discussion and feedback on your pieces from listeners. Always remember that music is composed to be listened to. Try to arrange performances of your work, whether it's a quick play-through with a group of friends or a formal concert with a paying audience.

## Arranging performances

Here are some ideas for getting your music played.

Compose for the instruments available in your class. This may just be keyboards and percussion, or you may be able to call on the help of a few people learning orchestral instruments. When you feel a bit more ambitious, write something for the school orchestra. You could start a group specially for the purpose of playing through student compositions, and even set up a composer's workshop during a lunchtime, when pieces could be performed and discussed.

If a piece turns out to be particularly successful, perhaps a group from your school could tour it round some other local schools. Or it could be played at a charity concert, or on local radio. Your teacher will be able to find out about youth orchestras and ensembles in your region, and you could try contacting them to see if they are interested in giving your work a performance. Many professional orchestras now have schemes in which players visit schools. Your school may be able to organize a visit of that sort.

If you are interested in theatre or dance, get your teacher to talk to colleagues about the possibilities of writing for a school production. If your school does not have a drama or dance department, try a neighbouring school or a local theatre or arts centre. Your local Youth Service may also run a youth drama or dance group.

A lot of popular music tends to be composed and played by bands whose members are a closed circle of friends. This can present problems for the lone songwriter trying to get his or her songs played, so why not suggest that your teacher sets up a 'session band' – a group of pop musicians prepared to meet and play other people's material, rather like professional session musicians.

If you are interested in composing music with a technological basis – electro-acoustic music or techno pop – try to get as much time as you can using the available equipment. It may be possible for your teacher to arrange a visit to a local studio.

## Be professional

If you expect people to play your music and to take you and your work seriously, you will have to cultivate a professional attitude. Make sure you plan rehearsals and ensure that the players have something neat to read. If you are not providing written-out parts then at least provide clear instructions. Obviously, there will be occasions when you will need to clear up a detail, but the players should not be expected to do your composing for you. Two common remarks are:

> "How do you want this piece to end?"
> "You've written a note which isn't on the instrument."

Both are quite embarrassing, and both are easily avoided by preparing yourself (and your compositions) properly.

# *First Steps*

CHAPTER ONE

# Giving your ideas a focus

Learning to be a composer sometimes involves working through exercises, and this book will provide plenty of opportunity to do that. But what happens when you try to use what you have learnt to compose a complete piece, with only the ideas in your head to guide you? This is something the beginner finds difficult, but it gets easier if you listen to lots of music and develop ideas you can draw on.

This chapter is about inspiration. One popular idea of inspiration is a gift or vision in which the composer hears music by magic. Unfortunately this only happens to composers in the movies. Inspiration does exist, but it is something you need to work at. Most professional composers have a reason for writing – usually because their music is intended for a purpose, like background music for a film or play, or because something catches their interest and suggests a piece.

Here are some possible sources of inspiration, with examples of pieces which have grown from them.

## Art and sculpture

Paintings can suggest scenes and stories, moods, forms and structures. One Swiss painter, Paul Klee, had a fascination for music, and wrote about the links between music and visual art in a number of books. Some of his paintings have musical titles; *Fugue in Red*, in which he explores the relationship between lines on the page and lines of music, and *Polyphonic Setting for White*, in which loud and soft are translated into foreground and background. In turn, Klee's pictures and ideas have inspired some composers, including Maxwell Davies, Schuller and Birtwistle.

The Impressionists were a school of painters, including Cézanne, Gauguin and Van Gogh, whose paintings were intended to *suggest* a scene, rather than depict it precisely. There are also examples of impressionism in music – for instance, some of the music of Debussy (listen to the *Préludes* for piano, the *Nocturnes* and *La Mer*).

There are many painters whose work suggests abstract structures. Mondrian and Matisse both manipulate blocks of colour, like the varied sections of a piece of music. 'Kinetic sculpture' is a type of sculpture which features movement using machines, mobiles and wind chimes. Sometimes the movement is random, suggesting ideas revolving dreamily in space; at other times the movements are rhythmic and repetitive.

## Architecture

The connection between architecture and musical form goes back into history. Some buildings have inspired an entirely new type of music – for example, the church of St Mark, Venice, which has galleries arranged around a central area. The potential for placing groups of instruments in opposite galleries, and writing pieces with echo effects, was exploited by composers in the late sixteenth century, such as Giovanni Gabrieli. Interest in St Mark's was revived by Stravinsky almost four hundred years later, in *Canticum Sacrum*, which consists of five main sections corresponding to the five galleries of the building. Several works by Stockhausen exploit architectural space, by involving instrumental groups or loudspeakers placed in different parts of the concert hall.

## The theatre

The most obvious link between drama and music is in opera. Although a full-scale opera is perhaps too ambitious an undertaking for the inexperienced, there are examples of more manageable forms.

**Ballad opera** (and its German equivalent **Singspiel**) was rather like the modern stage musical: arias and songs interspersed with spoken dialogue. The **dramatic cantata** was a type of mini-opera involving a small number of characters and a simple story. The **masque**, although large-scale in itelf, was an assembly of individual songs, dances and instrumental items around a common theme.

Plays provide numerous opportunities to compose music. This could take the form of an **overture** at the beginning, to set the mood or scene and settle the audience down, or **incidental music**, sometimes used between acts to 'fill in' while the scenery is changed, or sometimes featured as part of the play itself, for example music for entrances, exits, processions, dances and banquets.

Dance can be interesting for composers because it covers so many styles – the Baroque dance suite, classical ballet, contemporary, ballroom, jazz, disco, hip-hop and even circus and gymnastics. Composing for dance can be done in two ways; starting with the music and adding the dance, or starting with the dance and adding the music. Generally musicians prefer the first and dancers prefer the second. Some hints on composing for theatre, dance and especially TV are included in Chapter 6.

Some composers have drawn inspiration from the theatre in other ways. Fruitful links have developed in music theatre, especially deriving from two pieces, Schoenberg's *Pierrot Lunaire* and Stravinsky's *The Soldier's Tale*, both of which involve singers or reciters in costume acting out the text or story with the musicians on stage. The emphasis is generally on simplicity and 'low budget' techniques using masks and puppets, effective lighting and projected slides. *Master Peter's Puppet Show* by Falla is an example of a small-scale work using marionettes, and there is much to be learnt from the operas of Benjamin Britten (particularly *Noyes Fludde* and *Curlew River*) which, because they were composed for small performance spaces, are dramatically simple and compact.

## Film, television and broadcasting

The media provide a wealth of opportunity for composing music to order, ranging from short, snappy jingles to complete scores for silent movies.

Film and TV (and also dance) impose a very special discipline; having to compose music of a particular duration, and whose form is dictated not by considerations of musical structure but by the visual content. How this is done is explained in detail in Chapter 6.

Radio adverts and jingles can be fun to compose because of the scope to use the imagination. An historic battle scene featuring two warring armies would be extremely expensive to film, yet quite cheap to suggest on the radio using music and sound effects.

[2]

## Literature

Literature has inspired a great deal of music – most obvious in the countless cases when composers have either set poems or texts to music, or depicted a story in the form of a *tone poem* (see Chapter 12).

One problem associated with setting poetry is that if the poem or its translation is in copyright, you will need to obtain permission to reproduce it or perform it in public. The problem can be sidestepped by choosing non-copyright material.

Stories and texts drawn from the supernatural, mythology and religion have always been favourites with composers. More recently they have drawn upon strip cartoons (Berberian's *Stripsody*), nursery rhymes (Tavener's *Celtic Requiem*), political slogans (Henze's *The Long and Tedious Path to the House of Natasha Ungeheuer*), Nordic runes (Peter Maxwell Davies' *Stone Litany*), graffiti and newspaper cuttings (hip-hop and rap).

## Science

Science and music are closely linked through the study of acoustics and electro-acoustics. This can range from pieces which exploit acoustic phenomena (wavelength, amplitude, timbre, echo and reverberation, etc.) to pieces which employ tape recorders, keyboard synthesizers and other electronic equipment. Electro-acoustic music is discussed in Chapter 15.

Nature is another fruitful source. A number of composers have written pieces based upon the sounds of animals, including birds (Messiaen) and whales (Kate Bush). Harrison Birtwistle's *Medusa* (now withdrawn) consisted of melodies and ostinati based on the symmetrical form of the jellyfish, and it is also thought that Bartók's fascination for the proportions of the Fibonacci series (see Chapter 14) were the result of observing the structure of the pine cone (the sections and spirals of which are also arranged according to this series).

Astronomy has inspired a number of pieces, though in a fanciful rather than scientific way. The most famous is Holst's *The Planets*, and many more compositions have drawn ideas from astrology and the signs of the zodiac, making use of mystical ideas as well as the mathematical principles with which the signs are associated.

## Geography

Geography can provide a starting point for the study of world music. As you will see later on, techniques drawn from other musical cultures can usefully be adopted, or adapted, in your own compositions. A study of the rhythms of Latin America, not forgetting African drumming, will greatly help your understanding of pop rhythms, and a surprising number of world music styles can be successfully reproduced using European orchestral instruments, school percussion and electronic instruments.

*Gamelan* music from the Indonesian islands of Java and Bali has become popular in recent years. (The gamelan is a large percussion orchestra featuring gongs and metallophones.)

Indian classical music is hard to reproduce without authentic instruments, but popular music from India and Pakistan is now beginning to influence popular music in England, especially in the form of **bhangra** (a mixture of Indian film music and Western popular dance) and **ragga** (a mixture of bhangra, reggae, rap and technology).

## Mathematics

Maths is the basis of many musical ideas, especially rhythm patterns and minimalist structures. Mention has been made above of Bartók's interest in proportions, and this was also a feature of medieval music (see **isorhythm**, Chapter 14). It is also possible to employ mathematical principles in the design of the score of a piece, particularly if it is a graphic score featuring patterns and grids, and you will see in the section on twentieth-century techniques how twelve-note rows can be set out and varied using numerical formulae.

## History

History can teach us ways of approaching the styles and culture of a particular period, taking in authenticity of performance. (For example, is it correct to play Bach on a modern piano?) However, we need to make a distinction here: between those compositions which are inspired by studying the history of music, resulting in pastiche style studies, and those which are inspired by social or political events, like Tchaikovsky's *1812 Overture*. Generally it has been the vivid features of history which have attracted the attention of composers: disasters and conflicts, wars and revolutions, voyages and discoveries.

## Current affairs

Composers vary in their response to the big moral and political issues of the day. Some tend to be politically neutral; for example, Penderecki's *Threnody for the Victims of Hiroshima* depicts the horror of nuclear weapons but makes no particular political point. On the other hand the German composer Henze has stated that he is a communist, and many of his pieces reflect his political views in their choice of text. Since the 1980s punk rock, reggae and rap, have addressed issues like class, race, sex, unemployment and the environment, sometimes in a most forceful way. A number of pop stars have allied themselves to various campaigns and charitable activities.

## Festivals, customs and folklore

This is a very rich source of ideas because of the potential for combining music with other art forms. Examples could easily fill a book, but include the maypole and harvest festivals, the solstices, Advent, the Mardi Gras, the saints' days and, obviously, the big religious feasts and festivals: Passover, Ramadan, Christmas. Religious and recreational occasions drawn from other cultures include the Chinese New Year, the Australian Aboriginal Coroboree (a communal story and song festival with food) and the Wayang (an Indonesian shadow puppet show and party for the village community).

Composing religious music is a profession in itself. A great deal of music is specially composed for use in churches, temples and mosques, while other compositions are inspired by the composer's own faith, even though intended for concert performance.

## Games and sports

There are several examples of composers having been inspired by games. Chess has been made into a musical, and swimming has provided material for a number of ballets, including the very amusing *A Waterless Method of Swimming Instruction* by the London Contemporary Dance Theatre. Football and snooker have also provided material for musicals, although generally the true subject is a 'backstage drama' between the characters rather than an attempt to suggest the game itself in musical terms – although this is achieved in *Yale–Princeton Football Game* by Ives and *Rugby* by Honegger.

## Other musical ideas

Being inspired by other pieces of music is quite common, and many composers would admit to having been influenced in some way by the music they admire. Composers in their early careers often write music which is similar in sound to that of their teachers.

Generally influences tend to be subtle. Much of the music of Peter Maxwell Davies is composed using techniques drawn from medieval music. Steve Reich's minimalist music uses phrases which are closely related to rock guitar riffs. Yet Maxwell Davies' music does not generally sound medieval, and Reich's music could not be regarded as rock.

Obviously you should, as a composer, listen to as much music as possible, analyse it so you understand how it works, and try to focus your ideas about what sort of music *you* want to write. There is a danger of becoming so heavily absorbed in other people's music that you lose sight of your own identity. That's the time, perhaps, to go back to writing exercises for a while to develop your skills and confidence.

# CHAPTER TWO

# Games and Graphics

Having a composition performed in front of others can be like having to make a speech. Not everyone likes sharing their thoughts and feelings, and there is always a fear that your musical compositions might expose more than you feel comfortable about. Games and improvisations make it possible to contribute small ideas as part of a group where there is safety in numbers. The result may not always be satisfactory, but there is much to be gained musically by discussing what is wrong, and by finding ways of making improvements.

Most pieces which use graphic notation introduce an element of improvisation. Whether you compose a graphic piece by yourself or as part of a group, the responsibility for the end result will not be yours alone. There is less to feel shy about because there is less of you on show.

## Exercises using words

Words are a ready-made source of sound and rhythm. A wide variety of exercises and compositions can be made using repeated words and phrases. The words could draw on a common theme — for example names, places, clothes or food. The examples below are taken from the breakfast menu:

To produce a performance, start with a group seated in a circle. Each member chooses an item of food, to be repeated rhythmically and in time with a pulse set by a foot-tap or clap. The performance works best if members of the group enter one by one, allowing the texture to build up.

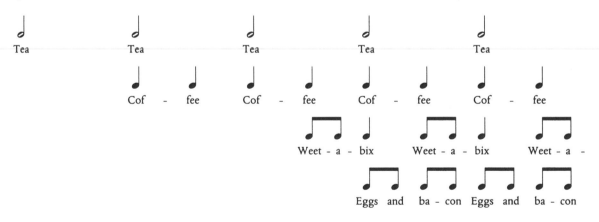

Think about your ending, too. The obvious thing is for the performers to drop out one by one. Can you think of other possible endings?

Once this can be performed fluently, your group could try to compose a piece for another group to perform. Try writing out the words with the note values, to see how the phrases might be notated.

The possibilities are endless, but on the next page are two ideas which should help explore counterpoints and textures. (This is taken further in Chapter 5.)

The first piece uses the names of the horses in a race. Each performer takes the part of a horse and the texture builds up to suggest the horses passing the winning post, with the leader first, followed by the main field, and finally the stragglers:

## Grand National

For the second piece you will need a street map. Devise a route from one place to another, then take the names of the streets you pass through, write them down and practise speaking them in a rhythm. Trace the route in the form of a rap. Then try combining this with an alternative route. When London taxi drivers take their test (called 'the knowledge') they have to recite the quickest route between two places sprung upon them by the examiner. The format is brisk and efficient; directions are 'right', 'left' and 'forward'. A typical journey might be expressed like this:

## Route Map
### From Elephant and Castle to Piccadilly Circus

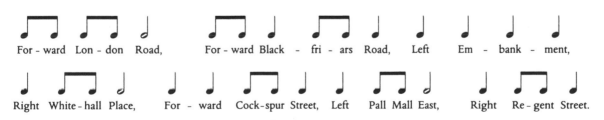

Not all compositions using words have to be based on rhythm; they can exploit timbre instead. Nor need they necessarily use complete words, with meanings. The next example (at the top of the next page) consists of one line of music for several performers singing a steady note. It begins with a vowel sound, progresses to sustained consonant sounds, then returns to vowels. Performers can either begin together (which will produce interesting results as they all get slightly out of step with each other), or they can enter one at a time, like a round.

# Ah-ooh

*AAA_____ OOO_____ MMM_____ ZZZ_____ LLL_____ AAA*

Try to hold a steady sung note while you make the sounds. See if you can all sing the same note. Hold the first sound for about 10 seconds, then take a quick breath and move on to the next sound. If desired, make the sounds through wind instruments or down tubing (e.g. the cardboard rolls used for sending posters through the mail). An added advantage of using instruments is that they provide something to hide behind if you feel shy about singing.

---

**More Ideas**

Here are more ideas for compositions based on words:
▶ Try pieces based on football chants, or announcements at railway stations or airports.
▶ Try chants made from the slow, sleepy speech of the hypnotist.
▶ Try compositions based on prayers: the responsorial psalm from the Catholic mass, or the Mantra, a Hindu chant.

---

## Making simple scores – cut-outs and collages

There are many sources of words, each with its own jargon and syntax: newspapers and magazines, cartoons and comics, football chants, graffiti, legal documents, instruction manuals, telephone directories.

With a pair of scissors and some glue you can compile scores. The following example is a three-part fugue; the subject is a newspaper headline whilst the other counterpoint material is drawn from the rest of the article. The rhythms are included for guidance.

### Rescue Drama

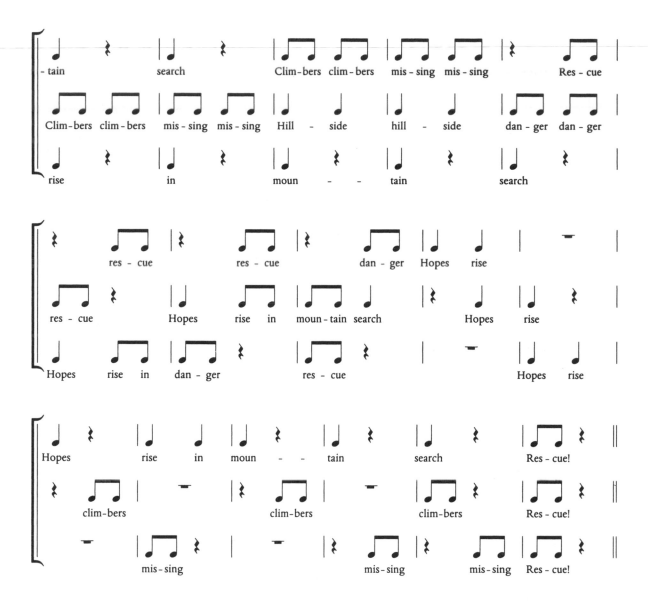

---

**More Ideas**

► Try cutting up and jumbling two very different sources of words, like a recipe and a set of regulations.

► Write out words and then cut them into syllables. Write a piece for several performers with the syllables distributed at random. (This is similar to a process in early music called **hocketing**.)

## Exercises using clapping and counting

One of the problems with vocal work is that it is quite hard to maintain a count in your head while you are speaking. It is easier to count when you are clapping, however.

One simple clapping and counting game is based on the idea of clocks ticking out of sequence with each other.

The performers are each given a number of beats to be counted over and over in their head. Performer 1 counts from 1 to 5, performer 2 counts from 1 to 7, performer 3 counts from 1 to 9 and so on. Everyone claps on 1 and the result is a series of independent handclaps.

The performance works best when the individual counts are quite long (i.e. avoid too many people counting 3s and 4s). You may find it helps to count in time with a beat provided by a percussion player or drum machine.

Performer 1, counting 5: **1** 2 3 4 5 **1** 2 3 4 5 **1** 2 3 4 5 **1** 2 3 4 5 *etc.*
Performer 2, counting 7: **1** 2 3 4 5 6 7 **1** 2 3 4 5 6 7 **1** 2 3 4 5 6 7 *etc.*
Performer 3, counting 9: **1** 2 3 4 5 6 7 8 9 **1** 2 3 4 5 6 7 8 9 **1** 2 3 4 5 6 *etc.*

This idea can be extended to make pieces based on rhythmic phrases. First, each performer devises a phrase by thinking of some words, putting them together and clapping the resulting rhythm.

Tea,    Cof - fee,    Or - ange Juice.

If you follow the format of the clocks exercise above you will arrive at the following structure. Here the single clap is replaced by a whole phrase:

*Player 1* claps his or her phrase once, then rests for the duration of the phrase (the best way to do this is to 'clap' the rhythm silently in your head), then repeats the phrase.

*Player 2* claps his or her phrase once, rests for two phrases, then repeats.

*Player 3* claps his or her phrase once, rests for three phrases, then repeats.

*Player 4* claps his or her phrase once, rests for four phrases, then repeats.

## Improvising with rhythm

One way of learning how to improvise pop rhythms is to practise clapping **fills**. Fills are the decorations added by a rock or jazz drummer, usually at the end of a phrase or leading into a chorus.

Devise a simple repeated pattern, perhaps on drums or keyboards. In place of every fourth repetition, have a gap like this:

‖: pattern | pattern | pattern | *(gap)* :‖

Next, every time the gap comes round, the members clap something to fill it. The example below is a simple rock drum pattern, repeated for three bars with a fourth bar silent for an improvised fill.

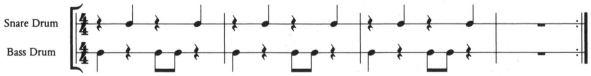

Once everyone gains confidence the fill can be made longer. Rhythms improvised in this way can form the basis of a composition. Practise and remember your patterns; they can provide material for composing counting pieces along the lines described above. They can also be used to invent ideas for melodies and riffs in the next chapter.

## Graphic scores

The word 'graphic' means, quite simply, 'written', but in contemporary music the term usually refers to a type of notation based on pictures, diagrams and graphs rather than staff notation.

Graphics in their simplest form can be employed to suggest the feel, rather than the details, of a passage of music. Obviously the players have a very important role since they are being called upon to interpret the symbols and improvise their own ideas. The example below is intended to prompt the performer to play something violent and jagged, followed by something smoother.

## War and Peace

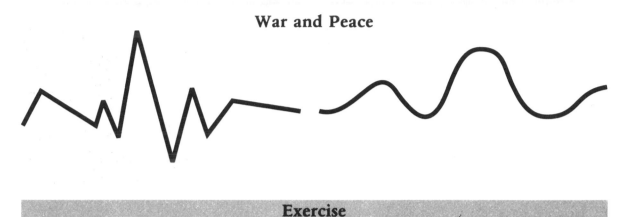

### Exercise

Placing graphic ideas in some sort of sequence represents a first step towards building a composition. One way to start is to draw four empty boxes and fill them with patterns and symbols.

Try to imagine what the end result might sound like: the mood of the music, the speed of the notes, and possibly whether they are high or low. The order in which the boxes are played can be left to the player.

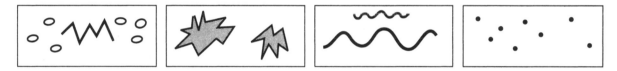

Arranging this composition for more than one instrument is quite straightforward – simply give a copy of the score to several players and ask them to start together, playing the boxes in an order of their choice.

You will, of course, have more control over the piece if you specify the instruments and when they are to enter. This might be achieved using a score based on a **track sheet** (for more on this see Chapter 8).

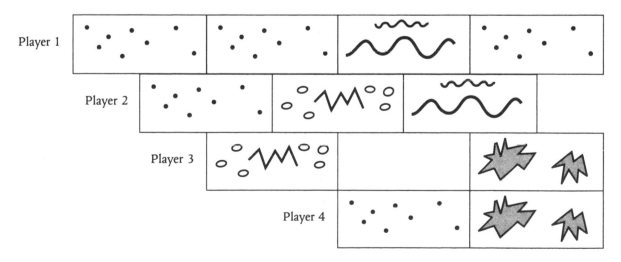

Pieces composed in this way will obviously have their limitations. Chapter 8 shows how graphics might be developed towards an understanding of staff notation.

► Try experimenting with symbols. Write out a piece and give the score to two different groups of players. Compare and discuss the differences in performance.

► Try writing a piece with a group of friends. Start with a sheet of paper divided into boxes (as in the example above). Each member of the group fills in one of the boxes, thinking about the nature of the music they are adding. Will it be the same as the previous section, similar or different? Will it be longer or shorter, faster or slower, louder or softer?

## Proportional notation

The main problem with the pieces illustrated above is that there is very little sense of ensemble; the players are working as individuals without much sense of what the others are doing. To provide this missing ingredient you could add a simple system of bars so that the material of one part can be synchronized with the material of another – as in the piece below, which is an example of proportional notation.

This piece is for four instruments – whatever is available: orchestral, keyboards, percussion, voices or a mixture of all four. Each bar is four seconds long, so by looking at the notes and the barlines you can see roughly how long each note should be held. You may need a conductor.

The notes are arranged on a one line stave. Notes above the line are high, notes below are low. It is up to the player to define *how* high or low, depending on the characteristics of the instrument.

The example is eight bars long. For the first four bars player 1 plays a simple melody (marked $f$) while the other three provide chordal support (marked $p$). In the last four bars player 4 takes the melody while the other three provide support.

### Quartet

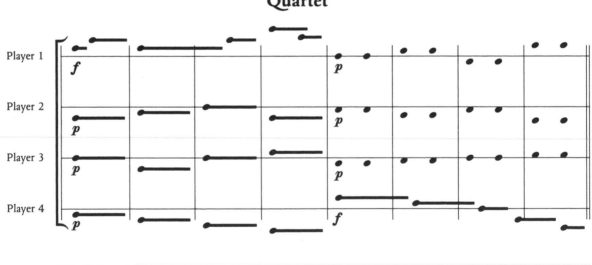

Compose a short piece using proportional notation. Try to focus your ideas – don't just put dots on the page and hope for the best. Think about the feel of the piece. Do you want it to be sad, dance-like, rhythmic? Do you want all the instruments playing at once or do you want more of a dialogue? Most important, listen carefully to the play-through. Is it what you expected? Did the players have any difficulty understanding your signs?

► Use proportional notation to compose a longer solo for one instrument (perhaps lasting about a minute). Add other instruments to provide a simple accompaniment. Add an introduction.

# Using dice, playing cards and dominoes

Compositions based on games of chance can offer a simple means of putting pieces together. The examples below can be performed by a small group (2–6 people) rather like an improvisation.

## Dice and board games

Most common board games can be adapted so the board takes the place of a score. The various sections on the board contain musical material geared to a range of abilities, and the players move from one section to another by the throw of a dice. The sections can contain a range of material from simple graphics to fully scored passages using the stave. The game can be played using voices, percussion or even wind instruments. The practicalities of throwing dice make the use of keyboards and strings rather more difficult, though not impossible.

The example below involves choices of route for the players. Start with a six.

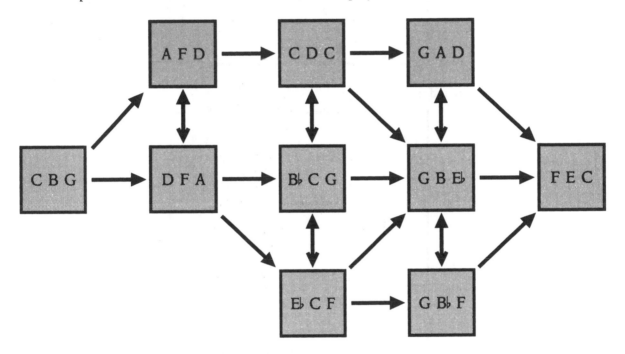

When players land in a box they play the notes indicated, in the form of a repeated phrase. Players choose their own rhythm and keep playing until their turn comes round again. The contents of the topmost box could be played in a number of ways:

The first player sets the general feel of the performance and it is up to the others to follow the mood, pulse, tempo, etc. This can be a useful game for developing ensemble playing, improvisation and leadership skills.

It may be necessary to limit the throw of the dice to one go every half minute or so; otherwise the musical performance may turn into a chaotic scramble.

▶ Games which progress from start to finish – snakes and ladders might provide some interesting variations:

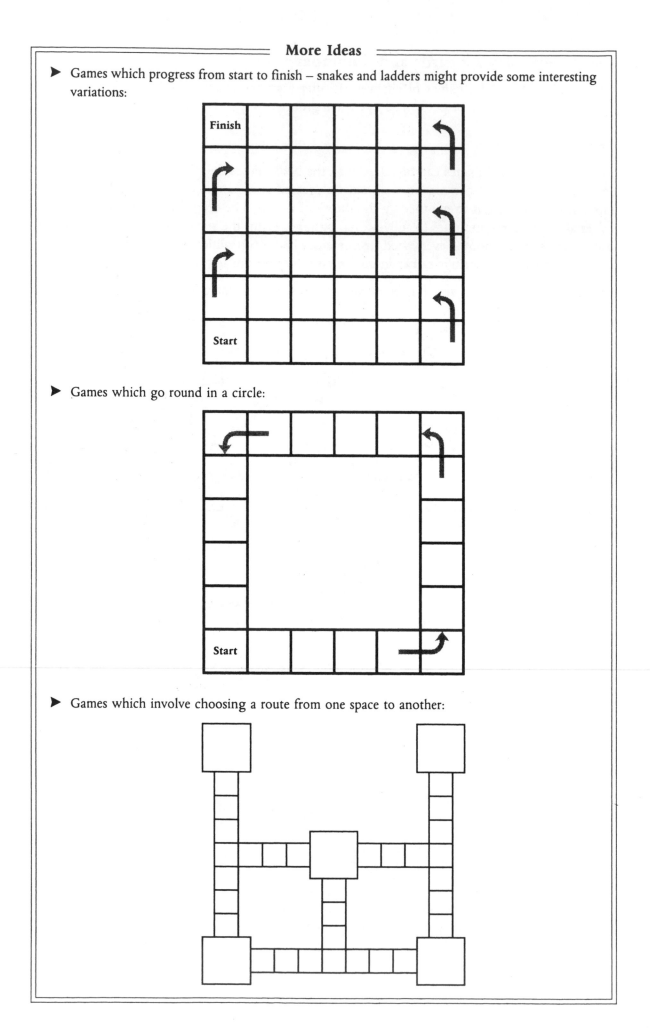

▶ Games which go round in a circle:

▶ Games which involve choosing a route from one space to another:

*Playing cards*

Playing cards are open to almost infinite adaptation, using the colours, suits or numbers in place of notated signs.

**Suits** can be used to identify instrumental groups, for example:
 ❤ percussion,   ◆ strings,   ♠ woodwind,   ♣ brass

**Colours** can represent loud or soft, fast or slow, play or tacet (silent).

**Numbers** can have a variety of functions:

▶ They can stand for bars or beats. For example number 7 could indicate 'play seven notes', 'play for seven bars' or 'silent for seven beats'.

▶ They could stand for the notes of a scale (a full suit of thirteen cards can conveniently be related to a full chromatic octave). A dealt hand could thus form a sequence of notes to be played as a melody or an ostinato.

## Exercise

A game of musical whist might be played as a group activity in which a hand represents a part. Here is one example:

The dealer removes 9s, 10s, jacks, queens and kings. The remaining cards from ace to 8 represent the notes of a scale. For example:

| C | D | E | F | G | A | B | C |
|---|---|---|---|---|---|---|---|
| ace | 2 | 3 | 4 | 5 | 6 | 7 | 8 |

Each player (with a xylophone or keyboard) is dealt a hand of five cards. The cards are kept in the order in which they were dealt, and translated into a melodic phrase. Each player repeats their phrase. The piece could be played in time with percussion or a drum machine, and the dealer could introduce 'variations' by dealing a new hand.

*Dominoes*

These can be useful in the planning or improvisation of a piece, because the dominoes contain up to twelve spots – one for each note of the chromatic scale. Sets could be arranged into melodies or **ostinati** (see page 47), or put together on the table to form a long melody (see also serialism, Chapter 13).

## Exercise

Each player is dealt six dominoes (remove the double blank). The spots are used to devise a set of notes based on a chromatic scale on C.

| C | C♯ | D | D♯ | E | F | F♯ | G | G♯ | A | A♯ | B |
|---|---|---|---|---|---|---|---|---|---|---|---|
| 1 | 2 | 3 | 4 | 5 | 6 | 7 | 8 | 9 | 10 | 11 | 12 |

Suppose one player receives dominoes whose spots add up to 4, 11, 5, 8, 6, 7. These correspond to the notes D♯, A♯, E, G, F, F♯.

The numbers can also be used to determine rhythm:

D♯ followed by 4 beats rest, A♯ followed by 11 beats rest, E followed by 5 beats rest.

A piece written for two xylophones using the above system might look something like this in proportional notation:

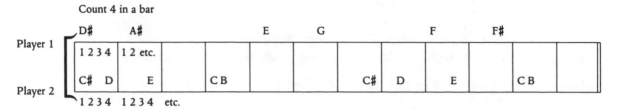

The next task is to add another section and extend the composition. Another round of the game will obviously produce another set of notes. Alternatively the set you have already could be put in a different order. More ambitious still would be an attempt to devise a new contrasting section. There are ideas about form in Chapter 6.

# CHAPTER THREE

# Melodies and Riffs

## A word about scales and modes

A working knowledge of scales is a big advantage in composing melody. To start with, here are a few basics.

The **pentatonic scale** is in many ways a gift to the beginner: the black notes of the piano (which make a pentatonic scale) are very easy to find and play; pentatonic melody has a way of bubbling along effortlessly; and, as we shall see, almost all pop riffs are pentatonic in origin.

Although the black notes of the piano are a convenient place to begin experimenting, their note names may be hard to remember. For composing purposes it may be better to use the white notes a semitone lower (C, D, F, G, A). You could also try out this scale on a xylophone, removing the bars you don't need (Es and Bs).

You should acquaint yourself with the **diatonic major scale**, particularly the first five notes which, as a beginner, you are recommended to use most often. This constitutes the so-called 'five finger exercise' because it fits under the keyboard player's hand. C major is the most accessible major scale on many instruments although guitarists may find E major more convenient. Each note has its own name (these are known together as the **degrees** of the scale). Time spent learning these will be rewarded later when you begin to construct chords and cadences (see Chapter 5).

A **minor** scale sounds sadder than a major one. You should start with A minor on the piano because it is made up mainly of white notes. Guitarists may find E minor easiest.

There are several forms of the minor scale, but the two below are perhaps the most useful at this stage:

**Harmonic minor** – with sharp *leading note* (now you know why you need to learn the degrees of the scale!):

**Blues minor** – so called because it is used as the basis for much blues and rock music. This has a *natural* leading note and consists, quite simply, of playing all the white notes on the piano from A to A:

The blues scale is an example of a **mode**. Other modes can be obtained, similarly, by starting on a different white note. There are thus seven modes available (including the major scale, which is one particular mode). Look them up in a music text book. Another mode worth learning is the one obtainable by playing all the white notes on the piano from G to G. This produces a major scale with a natural leading note – very common in pop music.

None of the excercises in this chapter will call for melodies to be composed in a particular scale or mode. To begin with you may find it helpful to start with the pentatonic scale or perhaps the first five notes of a diatonic one – but you need not stick to them slavishly. Only adopt rules and limitations if you think they will make composing easier for you; don't adopt them just for the sake of having rules.

## Composing melody

Melody is constructed rather like language; words fit together to form phrases, phrases form sentences, sentences form paragraphs and so on. This principle, of building up from small units, is the one which will be adopted in the excercises which follow.

Work a bar at a time. To arrive at your first idea you can try starting with the notes or starting with the rhythm.

### Exercise: compose a bar of melody starting with a repeated note

This method works well for people who may not be very skilled at counting beats and bars and writing down rhythms.

Imagine a note which keeps repeating – middle C. Try playing it. Add an accent to determine whether there are three beats in a bar or four.

Now take the first bar and start to alter the repeated notes, one at a time until you arrive at a melodic shape you like. The decisions are very straightforward: notes can go up, down or remain the same.

Having decided on an arrangement of notes keep it in mind – this is the first bar of your melody.

Invent one bar's worth of rhythm – you can tap it out on the table or, if you get stuck, you can try using the rhythm of words, or experiment with clapping (see the exercises in Chapter 2). Once you have your rhythm firmly fixed in your mind, play a repeated note in that rhythm. Now start altering the repeated note in the manner described in the exercise above.

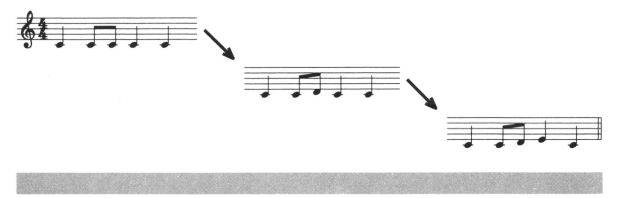

*Anacrusis*

An **anacrusis** is a weak beat at the start of a melody – in other words, the melody starts before the first bar:

Auld Land Syne

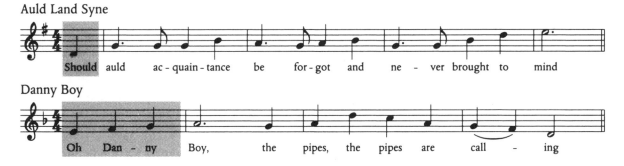

Should auld ac - quain - tance be for - got and ne - ver brought to mind

Danny Boy

Oh Dan - ny Boy, the pipes, the pipes are call - ing

Study some anacrustic melodies. They are not hard to compose, but you may find you lose track of the barlines when you come to build the melody up.

## Building melody

Once you have composed your first bar the remainder of the melody gets easier, for there are now only three courses of action: repeat the bar, vary it, or do something different. Many melodies tend to be in four-bar phrases. The form of these four bars tends to fall into a number of standard patterns. Some common ones are:

A A B A      A B A B      A A B C      A B A C

So if you wish to build an A A B A melody using your one opening bar, you need only compose one further bar (the 'B' bar) in order to complete the material needed for the whole phrase:

There are other ways of constructing melody than building up the bars like bricks in a wall.

## Exercise: compose a melody based on figuration

A **figuration** is the name given to a particular melodic shape.

Two very common figurations are scales and broken chords. (Don't worry at this stage why it's called a 'broken chord' – chords are explained in the next chapter.)

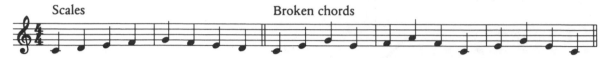

► Try composing a four-bar melody which uses a combination of figurations.

## Exercise: compose a melody based on an outline

Compose a four-bar melody by devising an 'outline' and then filling it in.

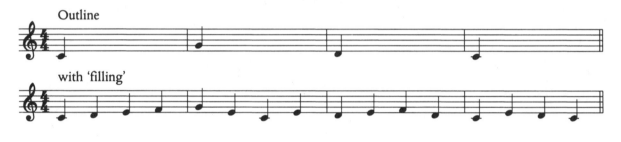

## Exercise: compose a melody based on a motif

A **motif** is usually a small melodic fragment. This is obviously a more intricate way of working, but it can provide a melody with a great feeling of unity and strength.

In the example below the first bar contains a simple motif in two parts, labelled 'a' and 'b'. This is worked into the other three bars. Note that it appears in different forms – transposed (shifted to a different pitch), backwards and upside down. Also, if you pick out the first note of each bar, you get the same melodic shape as the motif.

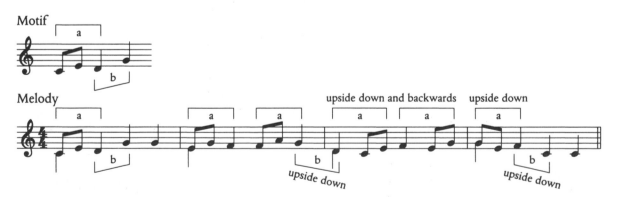

We will return to composing with motifs later in the book, because they can be a useful way of relating different parts of a large composition. If you want to read more about developing motivic phrases turn to Chapter 5, page 50.

➤ Try to give your melodies an identity. Try composing a simple march melody, a lullaby, a waltz, a spooky tune for a ghost movie.

➤ Try composing melodies for different instruments: violins, clarinets, recorders.

➤ Get your teacher to play some melodies by Haydn, Mozart or Beethoven. Pick out a short melodic motif and compose a melody of your own based on it.

## Extending melody

Having composed a four-bar melody you can now extend this into something longer. Think of your four bars as an opening phrase and try some of the ideas below.

### Repetition

The most obvious course of action is to apply the principle of repetition. The A A B A structure which was discussed above can be applied to **phrases** as well as to bars. Thus if we now refer to our four-bar phrase as 'A', we need to compose a new 'B' section, also four bars long. The resulting A A B A melody will then be 16 bars:

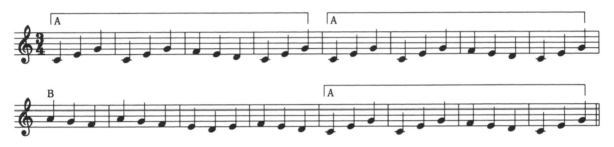

There are dangers in working to this formula, however. The above example has involved the composition of only five different bars. It is economical on ideas, which is a good thing, but it is perhaps too repetitive. This is the stage at which you might consider introducing some variation in the rhythm or melody. Most composers would do this in the final A sections:

A A B <u>A</u>     A A B <u>A</u>     C C D E     A A B <u>A</u>

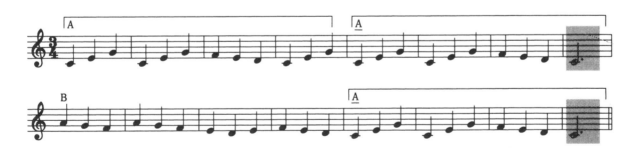

The extent to which you make alterations – whether you alter all the last bars or just some of them – is a matter for your own musical judgement. Don't be afraid of stopping the flow by introducing longer notes or rests. These will add breathing space.

## Sequences

A **sequence** is a short phrase which is repeated, but with each repeat starting on a different note. The Christmas carol *Ding dong merrily on high* contains one, on the word 'Gloria':

### Ding Dong Merrily on High

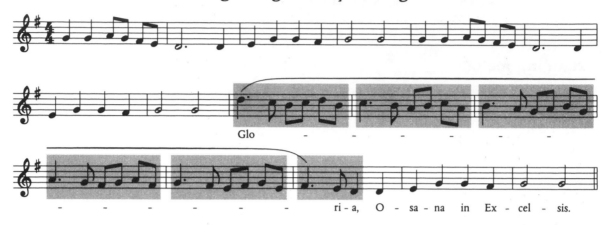

Sequences can be used to extend melody. Also, because they often give the impression of 'going somewhere', they can provide a sense of direction.

## Exercise: compose a sequence

In the example below a four-bar sequence is added to a four-bar A A B A melody. Two things have to be decided – the notes of the sequential phrase and what direction it will take: falling (commonest), rising (harder to compose) or dotted about (unusual).

Start by inventing an idea which contrasts with the opening material. This should be no more than a bar long. Then write it out three more times, each one starting a note higher or lower so as to form a chain.

While you are working, give some thought to where your sequence will end up. Note how the one in *Ding dong merrily on high* starts five notes up. By the time the melody has descended, it connects neatly with the final phrase.

Assembling the phrases may mean making a few adjustments until they fit like a jigsaw. The example below consists of a four-bar phrase, followed by a descending sequence which leads directly into a repeat of the opening.

*The importance of rhythm*

Melodies based on repeated rhythms can have a very strong structure, as well as being quite easy to compose.

Compose a melody using repeated melodic ideas and repeated rhythms. First, devise two bars of steady crotchet melody (A and B). Then devise two bars of rhythm (C and D).

Now make a four-bar plan. In the one below the melody takes the form AABA whilst the rhythm takes the form CCDD.

Note that in this example the number of notes in the rhythm is different to the number of notes in the melody. This is not a problem – simply repeat notes or leave them out as needs be to make things fit.

By adding rhythms and melodies together we get the following:

Melody:

Rhythm:

## Cadences

**Cadences** are used to punctuate music – either to bring a melody to a brief pause before going on, or to bring it to a stop. To use cadences effectively you need to know the degrees of the diatonic scale – particularly the first, known as the **tonic**, and the fifth, known as the **dominant**. Have a look at the scale on page 17 to refresh your memory.

Melodies which pause on the dominant have a sense of having arrived half way, with an expectation of continuing. This type of cadence is called an **imperfect cadence** – also (and not surprisingly) a **half close**.

Another type of cadence, the **perfect cadence**, usually appears at the end of a phrase and brings it to a halt. Typically the notes progress firmly from dominant to tonic.

The relationship between tonic and dominant is thus an important one; the dominant, when used carefully in a melody, can support the tonic and help to establish it as the key note.

However, the dominant is not the only note which can have this function – you can use the **leading note** or **supertonic** instead. These two notes, together with the dominant, make up the **dominant chord** (see also page 29). The use of these degrees of the scale will enable you to add variety to cadences, to extend melodies and give them a sense of forward drive.

(see also page 29)

## Exercises

Working with a partner, compose a four-bar melody but leave the fourth bar blank. Swap melodies and compose a cadence in the fourth bar. Swap back again and try to guess what type of cadence your partner has added.

Get your teacher to play some simple melodies (hymn tunes and folk songs will be suitable). Your teacher will pause each time there is a cadence. Try to guess what type of cadence it is.

Listen to (or play through) some Irish folk fiddle music. This is fairly easily obtainable from music shops and folk music suppliers. Much Irish dance music is based on repetition. See if you can compose a dance melody.

## Composing riffs

A **riff** is a short melodic phrase in a pop or jazz composition. Usually repeated as an ostinato, it can appear either in the lead part or in the bass or the backing instruments. Riffs are repeated, rather than building up like melodies with contrasting or varied ideas, and that makes them easy to work with. The only drawback is that because they use the syncopated rhythms of pop, they can be harder to write down than the melodies studied above. But don't be deterred: nearly all riffs are invented by pop musicians at their instruments and are remembered rather than written.

The techniques for composing riffs are much the same as those for melody.

## Exercise: compose a riff starting with the rhythm

Like drum patterns riffs tend to be either one or two bars long. You may find it helpful to compose riffs against a beat provided by a drum machine.

Interesting rhythms can be devised using the techniques discussed in Chapter 2. Get the rhythm firmly fixed in your mind first, then try playing it as a repeated note on an instrument. Gradually start to introduce new notes so the rhythm takes on a melodic shape. Keep it simple: lots of effective riffs consist of repeated notes and little else.

Much popular music is based on standard rhythmic patterns drawn from early jazz and Latin American rhythms. One of the most familiar is the one below, a pattern which underpins nearly all Latin rhythm, providing a syncopated background beat to which other parts are added.

This rhythm was very popular with early rhythm-and-blues composers (particularly Bo Diddley) but also appears in other styles. Here are examples of how it can be turned into a riff:

[24]

Riffs tend to be based upon a limited number of intervals drawn from the pentatonic scale. One reason for this is that early blues musicians found it easier to use the black notes on the piano. If you experiment with these you will see how these notes can produce 'pop-sounding' patterns.

It is rare to use all five notes of the pentatonic scale in a riff. The following patterns are common:

And in the bass clef:

Try out different combinations of notes. When you are happy with the general shape, start to develop it by adding a rhythm. The best riffs are the ones which are not too fussy. Try playing the notes in the rhythm of a simple rock drum pattern.

     Choose a note and try repeating it.

Try playing longer riffs – firstly in a 'straight' rhythm, then introducing syncopations. This practice was employed by early jazz players and is called 'ragging' (from which the term **ragtime** is derived).

straight

'ragged'

Here are some examples of two-, three- and four-note riffs.

Two-note riffs

Three-note riffs

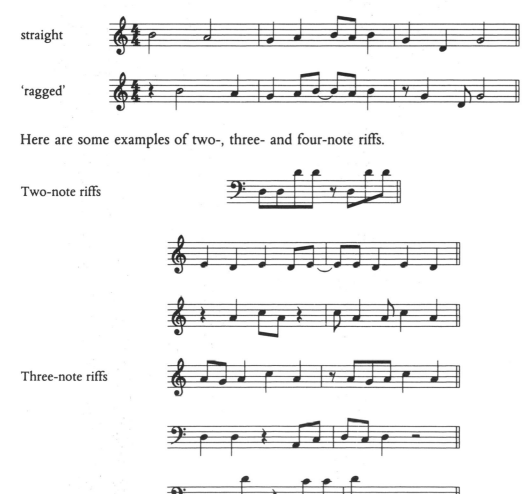

Four-note riffs

## Exercise: compose a longer riff using repetion

Repetition is often employed to give riffs a strong and memorable structure. Many two-bar riffs consist of a set of notes which is the same in both bars, but with varied rhythms.

Alternatively, the notes are varied and the rhythm is the same.

Many riffs are simply repeated over and over, but one common way of building a riff into a longer phrase is to transpose it. In the following example a two-bar riff is repeated a tone lower, making a four-bar phrase.

Experimenting with different transpositions is one way of arriving at a complete melody or even an entire verse of a song, but the riffs will have a stronger sense of direction if you think about the chords which might go with them. This is dicsussed in the next chapter.

# *Second Steps*

CHAPTER FOUR

# Chords

If you have worked through Chapter 3 you should have a clear idea about constructing melodies and riffs. To extend these ideas into longer compositions you will need to learn how to do two things: one is to add something to go with the melody or riff – perhaps an accompaniment or backing; the other is to compose a new section which can be joined on to the one you already have. These skills are covered in the next two chapters.

But, to be able to do either, you must first gain a knowledge of **harmony**, the way in which different sounds can be combined and related, and that is the subject of this chapter. It is also useful to familiarize yourself with the structures of some more scales in addition to the basic ones already covered. A knowledge of **intervals** is also important. An interval is the distance between two notes. Intervals take their name by measuring from one note to the other.

2nds, 3rds, 6ths and 7ths become minor when flattened.

The building block of harmony is the **chord**. A chord is a sound consisting of several notes played at once. Guitarists tend to find chords easy to relate to; they press down the strings on the fretboard with the fingers of one hand (the finger pattern is called a chord shape) and then strum the strings with the other hand. Each chord, and each guitar chord shape, has a name: for example C, D minor, G seven – although guitarists do not always know exactly what notes they are playing. Knowledge of the chord shape is enough to produce the right effect. In a similar manner some keyboards have auto accompaniment features which, at the push of a button, will play a chord in the form of a rhythmic pattern with drums.

However, you cannot always depend upon having a guitarist or keyboard available: you may need to know what the individual notes of a chord are so they can be used more effectively. This chapter is about the construction of chords, and some of the ways in which different chords can be played one after another to form **chord progressions**. (The term **chord sequence** is also sometimes used, but is avoided here so as not to confuse it with the melodic sequence, discussed in Chapter 3.)

## Triads

The simplest and most commonly used chords are called **triads** because they contain three notes.

Each of the three notes has a name: the bottom note is known as the **root**, the middle note the **third** (because it is three notes up) and the top note the **fifth** (because it is five notes up).

A triad can be built on any note. Below you can see a series of chords built on the notes of the major scale (C major in this example). The chords built on the minor scale (which are more complicated) will be covered later. On each degree of the scale is a three-note chord, each one taking its name from that degree. It is customary to number the degrees in Roman numerals.

The tonic chord is known as I, the supertonic as II, and so on. An important question is whether to refer to chords by their note name (as a guitarist would), or by Roman numeral. There are advantages and disadvantages to both approaches.

Calling a chord by its letter name is common amongst pop musicians, who invariably represent chords by **chord symbols**. These provide most of the essential information about the chord and the advantage is that, so long as you know what to play in order to produce the chord required, you can perform most songs without much technical knowledge of harmony. The disadvantage is that chords learnt in this way tend to be learnt in isolation; whilst you may know your scales (an essential skill for any composer!) you may still find it hard to translate the chords into another key because chord symbols give no clue as to how chords are related.

Roman numerals, on the other hand, can be applied to chords no matter what key you are in. For example, a twelve bar blues could be described as using only chords I, IV and V. Assuming you know your scales, you should be able to find these chords in any key. Roman numerals are used in the study of 'Classical harmony'. The disadvantage is that although they are clear enough when you use basic chords from the diatonic scale, the numerals can become very confusing if the chords get complicated (as they do in jazz), or if the piece modulates into a different key.

In the text below you will encounter both systems.

## Constructing triads

As you can see in the above examples, the triad has a characteristic shape, being built on alternate notes of the scale (and thus, if you are in C major, alternate white notes on the keyboard).

The interval separating each note of the chord is a **third** (because it is three notes away). The examples above contain two types of third, major and minor. A major third is the larger, being four semitones wide (i.e. four adjacent white *and* black notes). A minor third is smaller, being three semitones wide.

The way in which major and minor thirds are arranged in a triad determines what type of triad it is. In a major triad:

> ▶ from root to third is a major third
> ▶ from third to fifth is a minor third

i.e. the larger interval is at the bottom and the smaller at the top.

minor 3rd
major 3rd

In a minor triad:

> ► from root to third is a minor third
> ► from third to fifth is a major third

i.e. the opposite to the major triad: the smaller interval is at the bottom and the larger at the top.

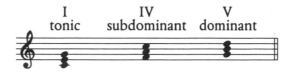

In the major scale there are three different types of triad. Chords I, IV and V are all major and are known as the **primary triads**. Many melodies can be accompanied using just these chords.

I  IV  V
tonic  subdominant  dominant

Minor chords tend to sound sadder then major ones. Chords II, III and VI are minor, and are known as the **secondary triads**.

II  III  VI

The remaining chord (VII) is **diminished**. A diminished chord consists of two minor thirds and is called diminished because the fifth has been lowered a semitone, from a perfect fifth to a diminished fifth. This chord is sometimes used in place of chord V.

## Chord symbols

Different types of chord have different chord symbols. A major chord is identified simply by its note-name (the name of the bottom note, or root), e.g. C, D, F. Minor chords have a small 'm' after the letter, e.g. Cm, Dm, Fm. Diminished chords say 'dim', e.g. Bdim. Further information can be included, such as any extra notes to be played in addition to those of the triad. More complicated chord symbols like these are covered in Chapter 17.

## Working with chords

There are two possible ways of devising a chord progression for a composition. One is to write your melodic ideas first and then find chords to fit. Another is to work out the progression of chords first and then build melodies on top.

### Exercise: adding chords to a melody

Start with a melody – either a well-known one or something you have composed yourself using techniques described in the previous section. All the examples below are in C major for simplicity, and you are advised to adopt this key to begin with unless you are feeling adventurous. If you are in any doubt about the key, here is a fairly accurate way of working it out: Look at the last note. This should be the point at which the melody feels as if it has come to a full stop. In most melodies this final note will be a note of the tonic chord, often the tonic itself.

Most melodies tend to suggest chords – this characteristic is called **implied harmony**. To work out the implied harmony you will, as a beginner, need to limit yourself to I, IV and V and work out what notes are contained in each chord. In C major they are as follows:

> ► Chord I consists of C, E and G,
> ► Chord IV consists of F, A and C,
> ► Chord V consists of G, B and D

Although these chords have some notes in common, it should not be too difficult to look at the melody, bar by bar, and work out which chord is most strongly suggested. Start by filling in the cadences. If you have read Chapter 3 you will remember that cadences are often clearly signposted in the melody.

Now select the other chords you think will fit and add them. Don't try to be too complicated; aim for one chord per bar and sustain it through that bar.

In addition to working out chords from the notes of the melody there is another method: trial and error. For example, in most compositions the first chord you hear is likely to be I. Therefore try chord I in bar 1.

You could also try chord I in bar 2 but it is more likely that this bar will involve a new chord. Try IV and V and keep the one which fits best.

Bar 3 will involve a similar choice between two chords.

## Exercise: Harmonize a melody using both primary and secondary triads

Although it is possible to harmonize most melodies with chords I, IV and V, you may encounter melodies with bars which seem to suggest something different, or you may wish to introduce some variety. Try experimenting with chords II, III and VI. These chords are each related to one of the primary triads because they have notes in common. For example, in C major:

- ▶ I (C, E and G) is related to VI (A, C and E)
- ▶ IV (F, A and C) is related to II (D, F and A)
- ▶ V (G, B and D) is related to III (E, G and B)

The secondary triads can therefore sometimes be used as substitutes for the primary ones. Here is the last example again, with some secondary triads added in place of the original ones:

=== More Ideas ===

Ask your teacher to help you find some melodies with simple harmonies: early rock 'n' roll songs (especially Buddy Holly or Chuck Berry), folk songs or nursery rhymes. Copy out the melodies and write above the stave, in chord symbols or Roman numerals, the chords you think will fit. If reading the music feels a bit too difficult, try writing out the lyrics and write in the chords above the words where you think a chord change occurs.

# The minor mode

The examples above were all in a major key. Working in the minor is slightly more complicated because there is more than one version of the minor scale. This means that there can be more than one version of some chords.

Building triads on the minor scale gives rise to four different types of triad. Major and minor will already be familiar, and diminished triads (comprising two minor thirds) have also been mentioned. The fourth type is the **augmented triad**. This is built from two major thirds, as in this example:

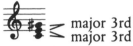

If you are trying to add chords to a minor melody, let your ear be the judge. You will have to learn some new chords with black notes. Here are some chords to choose from:

| | |
|---|---|
| I | minor |
| II | minor or diminished |
| III | major or augmented |
| IV | usually minor, sometimes major |
| V | usually major, but sometimes minor in pop and jazz |
| VI | major or diminished |
| VII | major or diminished |

Key – A minor

In many cases it is possible to harmonize minor melodies in two ways.

a)

b)

---

**More Ideas**

► Study some simple songs – perhaps from one of the popular busker's collections. Most anthologies identify the chords which are to be played. See if you can write out the chords in full.

► If you have a keyboard with auto-chord effect, try to produce a live performance with a friend. One of you can play the melody while the other enters the chord changes.

► Once you have composed a melody, try transposing it into another key and then add chords.

## Devising chord progressions

Working out the chord progression first is common practice among pop musicians: the chords often form the basis for an improvisation during which melodic ideas might be developed. However, this approach can also be applied to other styles – for instance, Baroque or Classical. Chord progression is what gives many styles their sense of direction.

Like melodies, chord progressions tend to be arranged according to a certain number of bars. Examples below are divided into two- and four-bar progressions and those of eight bars or more.

### Two-bar progressions

These are especially common in popular music although it is debatable whether a mere pair of chords is enough to be called a progression. Typically the two bars will be repeated over and over, one chord per bar, with a strong drum backing.

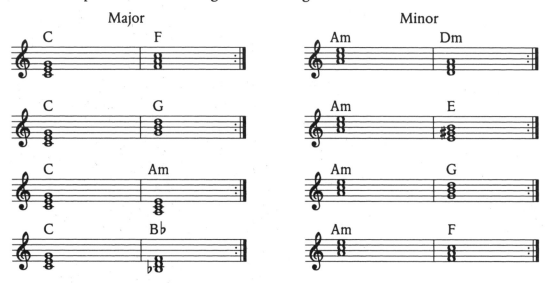

The pattern might be given some rhythmic articulation, so it can be played in the form of an accompanying riff, (there are more ideas at the end of this chapter).

Two-bar patterns can be very effective if there is more than one chord per bar, thereby creating an interesting **harmonic rhythm**. A great many variations are possible using only I, IV and V. Here are two examples:

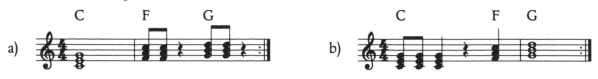

It is a relatively simple matter to turn such a pattern into a riff strong enough to form a memorable part of a song:

Choose a chord progression. It could consist of two chords only (one per bar), or you might decide to use three chords, with two of them fitting into one bar as in the examples above.

Now invent a rhythm lasting two bars. The easiest way to do this is to try tapping out the rhythm whilst counting 1 to 8. As soon as the rhythm is secure change your count to two bars of 1, 2, 3, 4.

Lastly, try playing the chords in the rhythm. Fitting them together may require a few adjustments, but keep experimenting until you are satisfied with the result.

=== **More Ideas** ===

Listen to some reggae. A great deal of reggae is based on two-bar chord sequences, typically one chord per bar (see Chapter 16). Try to work out the chords in a song, and play them on a keyboard.

*Four-bar progressions*

These form the basis of a great deal of music. The following progressions are common in many styles:

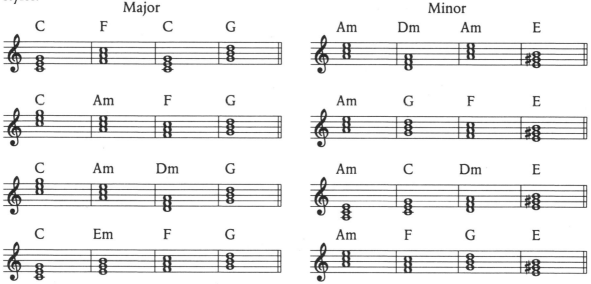

Some of the strongest progressions tend to involve chords whose roots are four or five notes apart, for example I–V, I–IV, VI–II–V–I — and II–V–I which forms a commonly used and very strong cadence.

Progressions between chords whose roots descend by a third are also strong, for example I–VI–IV and IV–II–VII:

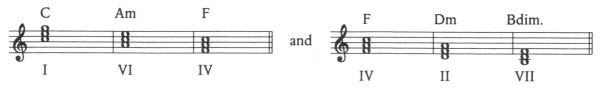

Stepwise chord progressions, for example I–II–III–IV, are common in popular music but rare in classical harmony.

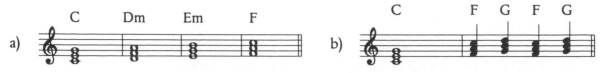

Many rock chord progressions are built around major triads on the pentatonic scale. Guitarists find these fairly easy, but if you play the keyboard you will have to learn some new chords with black notes.

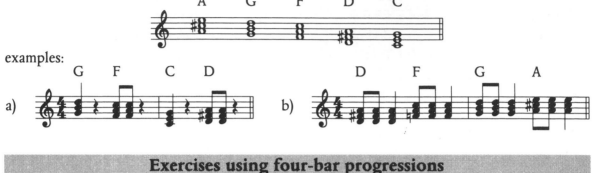

examples:

## Exercises using four-bar progressions

There are a number of techniques for constructing your own progressions, rather than relying on standard ones. One is to build around a cadence.

The following example is a four-bar progression ending with a perfect cadence – a progression from V to I. These chords will occupy bars 3 and 4. Since it is likely that the first bar will be occupied by the tonic, only bar 2 remains to fill:

You could also build a sequence around an imperfect cadence:

Another technique is to adapt one of the melody-building principles discussed in the previous section. Like melodies, chords can be can be composed around a structured formula. Do you remember these structures for building melodies: AABA or ABAC? (A and B here represent phrases or sections, or bars of melody – not names of chords.) Chord progressions can follow the same structures. For instance an ABAC structure might be played as a C–G–C–F chord progression.

But don't get confused by these different ways of using letters. The important point is that chord progressions can be based around patterns of repetition.

*Eight or more bars*

One of the simplest ways to compose an eight-bar progression is to join together two four-bar ones:

Alternatively you can construct your eight bars by chaining together smaller units. Here, a two-bar pattern is played three times with a different two-bar pattern added at the end, creating an overall AAAB structure. This one is a typical rock pattern, and is shown with a bass line:

It is important to decide where your cadences will be. The next example consists of four bars ending with a half close, followed by another four bars ending with a perfect cadence:

There are several longer examples of standard chord progressions. One of these is the twelve-bar blues. You should familiarize yourself with this as it forms the basis of much popular music but uses only I, IV and V:

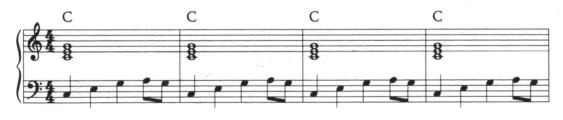

## Exercises using longer chord progressions

You will need several groups for this exercise, which involves building up a composition bit by bit.

Each group devises a chord progression of four or more bars. The chords are written down, either fully notated on the stave or as a list of chord symbols or Roman numerals. This is then passed on to the next group.

Each group now has to work out and play the chords they have been given, then devise a melody to go with them.

## Exercises using the twelve-bar blues

Compose a one-bar riff using one of the methods described in Chapter 3. Then construct a twelve-bar blues based on your riff, in the manner of the example below.

This blues is in D minor, and the first note of the riff is the tonic, D. If you follow this example your exercise should fall into place.

You will see below that the riff is transposed in accordance with the twelve bar chord structure. In bars 1–4 the riff starts on the tonic, D. In bars 5–6 it is transposed up four notes to the subdominant. In bars 7–8 it returns to the tonic. In the last four bars it follows these chords: dominant, subdominant, tonic, dominant.

When you have mastered the blues structure, try using it as a way of learning to improvise.

The blues in the example below is to be performed by two players (or groups of players). It consists of a simple call-response pattern. The written-out bars are played by one player, on a bass instrument or in the bass register of a keyboard. The blank bars are filled in by the other player.

This blues could also be copied out and used as a composing exercise. The object would be to complete the empty bars.

[36]

## Harmonic rhythm

Many of the examples so far have involved progressions of one chord per bar. This is a fairly easy format for the beginner to work with, but it is rather limiting. The frequency of chord changes, or **harmonic rhythm**, has an important effect on the pace of the music. In the example below the harmonic rhythm is varied: some bars have one chord, others two.

**Exercise**

Devise a four-bar chord pattern – but before you work out the chords, decide on a harmonic rhythm. Then fit chords to this rhythm.

## Inversions

A triad can be played with a note other than the root in the bass. Such an arrangement is called an **inversion**. In the chord of C major the inversions are as follows:

First inversion (with the third, E, in the bass)

Second inversion (with the fifth, G, in the bass)

Alongside the appropriate Roman numeral, a first inversion is is identified by a small b and a second inversion by a small c, e.g. Ib, Vc.

Chord progressions using inversions are very common in Classical harmony but tend to be rarer in popular music. When chord symbols are in use, an inversion is indicated by stating the bass note after the chord name. Thus C/E is the first inversion of a C major triad, and C/G the second inversion.

First inversions are more common than second inversions, which work best when subject to certain rules, (these are explained in Chapter 10).

Inversions can add enormous variety. They can give the impression of movement without actually changing the harmony:

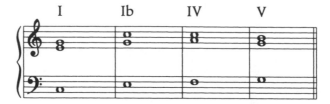

## Voicing

**Voicing** is the term used to describe the arrangement of notes in a chord, particularly which one is at the top. The term is used mainly by pop and jazz musicians. There are many ways of voicing a chord of C major in root position. In the following example the root is played on the piano by the left hand whilst the right plays a selection of different voicings:

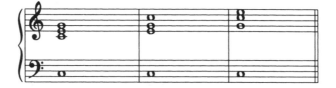

Attention to voicings will help to make chords flow from one to another. A chord sequence for keyboard which features only one type of voicing will tend to force your hand to leap about:

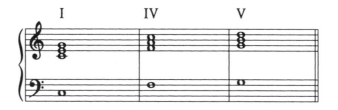

If the chords are voiced differently the hand will have less distance to travel:

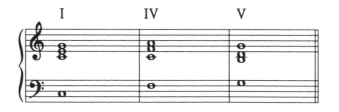

## Exercises

Devise a chord progression and try to arrange the voicings so the top line of notes moves by step as far as possible. Here's an example:

Devise a chord progression in root position. Now change some of the root positions to first inversions so that the bass line moves more smoothly.

Devise a four-bar progression. Now try writing it out in three parts – a melody on the top, a bass at the bottom and an inner part to complete the harmony.

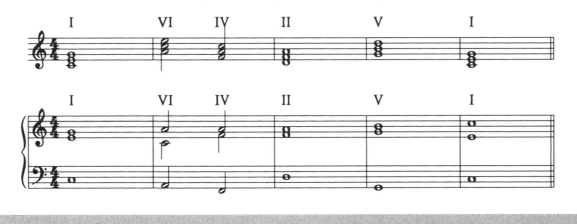

## Accompaniments and backings

If all chords were played at the beginning of the bar and held all the way through, music would be extremely dull. The art of accompaniments and backings is the art of articulating chords interestingly to give the music a feeling of movement. In the following example the chord progression C–Am–F–G is given simple rhythmic articulation:

You do not have to play a chord as a 'block'. An alternative is to suggest the chord in broken form, or as a repeated phrase, riff or figuration:

As soon as you feel confident in working out chords you should, as far as possible, try to make them interesting by adopting patterns like the ones above. However, the art of adding parts together is the subject of the next chapter.

# CHAPTER FIVE

# Textures

## Introduction

The word 'texture' in music refers to the way in which ideas are arranged in layers.

One of the simplest textures, a melody with a simple chordal accompaniment, was introduced in the previous chapter.

A simpler texture still is the melody and drone. This is common in much folksong and early music. Usually the drone is on the tonic, but in the example below the drone begins on the tonic and then switches to the dominant for contrast.

A well-known drone effect is provided by the bagpipes. Try arranging some Scottish dances for instruments, some playing the melody and some playing a tonic drone.

Another type of music employing drones is the music of the Australian aboriginal wind instrument, the didjeridoo. Listen to some recordings of didjeridoo music and see if you can compose a short piece for European wind or string instruments which copies the pulsing drone effect.

However, the drone is a very simple example of a texture. Music can become boring for the listener if there is not enough melodic or rhythmic life in the accompanying part. This chapter is about different ways in which parts can be added together to create more interest.

## Doublings

For centuries composers have employed a very simple device to thicken up melodies and give them more presence: doubling them. In the example below, a melody is doubled at the octave.

A richer effect is produced by doubling the melody a third above or a sixth below. These doublings are common in opera duets, and also in backing vocals in popular music.

There is a great deal of scope for doublings, especially when they involve two different instruments. For example, a common orchestral practice is to double a violin melody by the flute an octave higher.

Choose a melody and try some doublings:
> ➤ Try doubling the rhythm using a percussion instrument.
> ➤ Try different combinations of instruments.

The drawback with doublings is that the texture is always note-against-note. There is no independence between the two parts. A limited degree of independence can be achieved by adapting a doubling, perhaps by leaving out some of the notes and mixing the intervals:

## Counterpoint

For a greater degree of independence between parts it is necessary to write proper **counterpoint**, in which two or more separate melodies or melodic ideas are blended together. In earlier periods of music the training for student composers involved a the study of **species counterpoint**. You do not have to follow this course of study through all its stages here, but some features of it can be adapted to provide useful practice.

### Exercises

First, compose a melody in semibreves and add a countermelody, note-against-note. You will find that countermelodies above are easier to write than ones below, but you should work at both. Concentrate on the interval between the two parts, which should be a third, fifth, sixth or octave, but do not worry too much at this stage about what the implied chords might be.

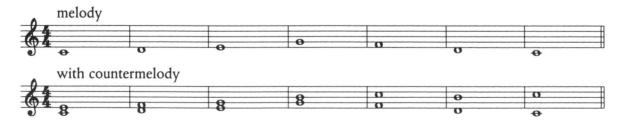

Now keep the first note of the countermelody and 'fill' the bar in, first with minims:

[42]

... then with crotchets:

... and finally with some quavers:

### Non-essential notes

You will find there are a number of options available when filling out a melody in this way.

Passing notes:

Auxiliaries:

These extra notes are called non-essential notes because they are decorative only, and do not form part of the chord.

---

**More Ideas**

► Choose a hymn or carol and compose a **descant**. This is an additional melody which fits above the main one. The words are normally the same as for the main melody.

► Write out a familiar tune in semibreves and compose a countermelody in quavers.

---

## Ground basses

One very effective texture is a two-part one consisting of a melody and a bass line, especially when the bass line is a repeated pattern. Such a bass is called a **ground**, or **ground bass**.

The term is usually associated with music from the Baroque period, although the principle can be applied to any style. A great deal of popular music is composed over a ground which may last four or more bars, or which may consist of little more than a short riff.

Compose a short two-part piece using a repeated bass line. Devise the bass line first, then add the melody.

Alternatively you can work out a chord progression and build the bass line around it. One way to do this is to place the root note of the chord on the first beat of the bar and fill in the other beats so as to create a steady melodic bass line. This is sometimes known in jazz as a **walking bass**.

When you are satisfied with the bass, try adding a melody. You may find it easier if you work with a partner.

## Rounds

You can probably remember singing 'Frère Jacques' and 'London's Burning' when you were young. These are examples of rounds.

Rounds are often written out as a single melody with an asterisk (*) to show where the voices enter.

The distance between one entry and the next is an important feature of a round. In many rounds this is two bars: when the first performer gets to bar 3 the next one starts, and so on.

## Exercise

Compose a round for instruments (or voices singing la-la).

Rounds are quite easy to compose provided you keep your ideas simple. Keep to the same harmony in every bar. Note that in the example below the first note of each bar is a note of the tonic chord. Also, each bar is repeated so as to produce an AA BB CC DD structure. Many rounds are based on this pattern.

You may find it helpful to write out the first notes of each bar before you compose anything else. This will provide you with a sort of skeleton which you can fill in. An eight-bar melody should be long enough for an interesting round.

## Canons

The principal differences between a round and a canon are as follows:

▶ In a round the same melody is repeated over and over – consequently the melody of a round tends to be quite short (rarely more than eight bars). A canonic melody tends to be longer.

▶ The harmony of a round is usually very simple, giving it a nursery rhyme or folk-like quality. The harmony of a canon is often more complicated.

▶ All the entries of a round are usually on the same note as the first entry. The entries of a canon can be at any interval.

For the inexperienced, composing a canon can seem rather painstaking, yet canons are very economical on ideas: you only have to compose one melody!

## Exercise

Compose a short canon in two parts.

When you compose your first canon follow these guidelines:

The greater the number of beats or bars between the entries the easier it is to compose. Four bars are easier than two, two are easier than one.

Avoid large melodic leaps and phrases which run up and down scales a great deal. This should avoid the possibility of parts crossing. Crossed parts do not necessarily mean that the canon will sound unmusical, but they can cause tangles which are hard both to perform and to write out.

For the same reason the interval of the canon – the gap between the note of the first entry and the note of the second entry – should be an octave (so that the second voice enters an octave higher or lower than the first started). A canon at the unison (where the second entry starts on the same note, like a round) could prove rather cramped.

Construct the canon interval by interval, and don't worry at this stage what the implied chords might be. Decide when you want your second entry to be and compose up to that point. For example, if you decide on your second entry starting after two bars, you will need to write a two-bar melody:

Now write it out on a stave above or below, to form the second entry:

You can now compose the next two bars of your canonic melody to go with the first two:

This is now written out in the second part, and another two bars added. The process can continue in this leapfrog fashion up to the end of the canon. You may need to plan the last two bars carefully so the canon can come to a convincing stop.

---

## More Ideas

► Study some examples of canon. One, which works in several parts, is Tallis' Canon (better known as the hymn *Glory to thee my God this night*). Bach was a master at canonic composition (see his *Two Part Inventions* and *The Art of Fugue*), and there is a wonderfully crafted canon which makes up most of the material in the last movement of Franck's *Sonata for Violin and Piano*.

► Try taking the first two bars of a well-known melody and using them as the basis of a canon.

## Ostinati

The word **ostinato** (plural *ostinati*) is Italian and means obstinate. In music it usually refers to something which is repeated over and over, usually a phrase.

Pieces based on ostinati tend to be easy and economical to compose because they frequently involve the repetition of simple ideas. Ostinati can also provide a sense of forward motion, especially if used as an accompaniment.

In the example above the ostinato figure was altered in bars 4 and 7 to suggest cadences. It is possible, however, for an ostinato to be repeated in a much more mechanical fashion, taking no account of what the implied chords might be.

## Exercise

Compose a pictorial piece using ostinati, called *Taking a Melody for a Walk.*

First, write a melody using long notes, such as semibreves. This may be repeated as often as you need to extend the piece.

Now compose a second part consisting of a succession of ostinati. Each ostinato should have its own character, and together they should suggest a simple story. The example below starts with heavy footsteps, then speeds up to a walk followed by skipping, then running.

[47]

## Minimalism

Some composers write music which is constructed using ostinati and nothing else: the music consists of repeated phrases and rhythms which interlock using techniques similar to those explored in Chapter 2 (see pages 6–9). This type of music is called **minimalist**. Minimalist composers include Terry Riley and Steve Reich (USA), Steve Martland and Michael Nyman (England), and Louis Andriessen (Holland). Because of its tendency to feature catchy rhythms minimalism sometimes suggests pop music. Another link with pop is the common use of pentatonic scales (see Chapter 2).

## Exercise

Some of the simplest minimalist compositions are performed like a round, the players being given a set of ostinati which they repeat.

The piece below consists of several simple pentatonic ostinati enclosed by repeat marks. Each player is given a copy although it is possible to work without a score provided the players are able to remember their parts.

There are a number of ways of performing this:

▶ The first performer plays up to the first repeat mark and continues to repeat bars 1 and 2. The exact number of repeats can be specified by the composer or left to the player. After completing the repeats the player moves on to the next phrase. Player 2 then enters at the beginning. When player 2 moves on player 3 enters and so on, building up into a thick texture.

▶ Everyone begins together. After a number of repetitions (each individual chooses how many) they move, one by one, on to the next phrase, the result being that the players get 'out of step' with one another.

▶ Everyone begins together choosing any phrase (not necessarily the first), moving on to another phrase as and when they choose.

It can be quite easy to spin out a long piece from only a few ideas. However, be careful not to overdo the number of repetitions: the simplicity of minimalism can be one of its dangers because it can produce some very dull musical landscapes.

---

### More Ideas

One common performing problem is keeping together. This can be solved by the addition of a part which is played throughout and provides a strong pulse: a bass line, percussion pattern or pop drum part. Alternatively you, the composer, could conduct, beating a simple pulse and perhaps indicating when each player should move on to a new phrase.

When composing ostinati for a minimalist piece try to think ahead; you need to arrive at a piece which not only builds up or unfolds in some way but also contains some variety.

Ostinati can incorporate a range of features:

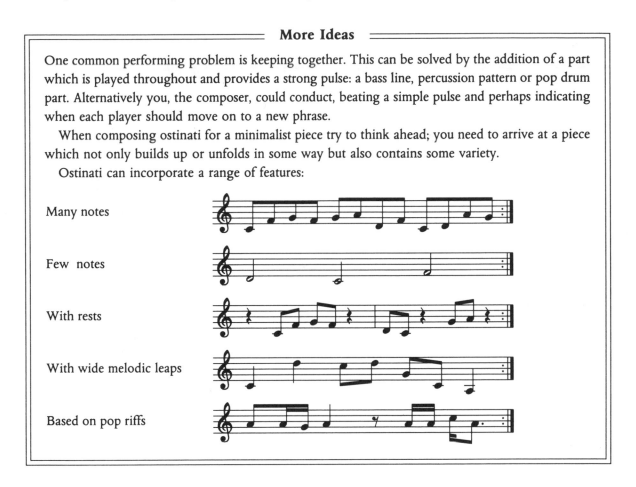

---

## Adding variety

When you have mastered the techniques above you should introduce ways of making your pieces more interesting, both to perform and to listen to.

### Rhythmic variety

Much minimalist music is based on **polyrhythm**. The principle of this was introduced in Chapter 2 (see pages 6–10). It is fairly easy to write polyrhythmic counterpoint – one way is to compose several ostinati, all of different length. What happens is that the various repeats of the ostinati begin to overlap once the players get going.

It may help to write out the ostinati one above the other, so you get some idea how their overlaps may sound.

Then they can all be written out end on end, and given to the players:

Another way of creating overlapping ostinati is to place rests of different lengths between each repetition:

The secret of performing polyrhythmic pieces is to avoid counting bars and simply tap your foot to the basic pulse.

## Melodic variety

Some mimimalist pieces involve the slow transformation of one idea into another. There are many ways of developing a phrase:

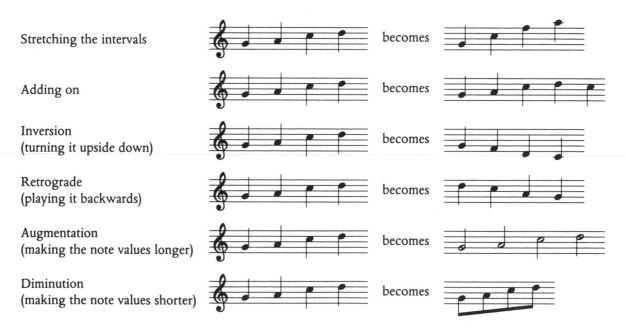

Stretching the intervals

Adding on

Inversion
(turning it upside down)

Retrograde
(playing it backwards)

Augmentation
(making the note values longer)

Diminution
(making the note values shorter)

## Other ways of introducing variety

Don't forget that you can vary the texture. Pieces can build up, with instruments entering one by one. Alternatively instruments can drop out to create a thinner texture.

In the music of the Indonesian *gamelan* – a large percussion orchestra whose music features ostinati – it is common to find different versions of the same ostinato being played at the same time. In the example below, each line is not only a variant of the other, but also features different note

values. The variations are achieved by introducing extra notes between the main ones. Thus, in the middle line **G    A    E    D**
becomes          **G B A C E C D** B.

## Exercise

Try composing a simple pentatonic ostinato and then add some variations to it in the manner of gamelan music.

---

#### More Ideas

Try writing a minimalist vocal piece based on the street cries of London. These were used by street sellers in the eighteenth and nineteenth centuries and are well documented in music history books. There is a part song based on them in the musical *Oliver*.

---

## Composing for instruments

Many of your composition exercises will be worked out at home or school using available instruments, probably keyboards or tuned percussion. But you should experiment with a wider range of textures as often as possible, composing for other instruments or perhaps even for a small ensemble or band.

This section is about scoring for orchestral instruments; pop instruments are discussed in Chapter 18. There is only space here to cover the basics, and you are strongly recommended to consult a book on orchestration which will give you details about the characteristics of each instrument and the ways in which they are blended together.

Instruments are divided into four main families: woodwind, brass, strings and percussion. The list below includes the most common in each of the families and identifies whether they play in the treble or bass range, or in between. Don't exceed the ranges given unless the players are very skilled. In any case, if you are working with young players or beginners it is always sensible to check what they are capable of.

On page 52, instruments are listed in the order they appear in an orchestral score, reading from top to bottom. Instruments marked * are called **transposing instruments**. Don't be deterred from writing for them if you are not sure how to transpose. Ask someone to help you. The instrumental ranges shown here are not transposed.

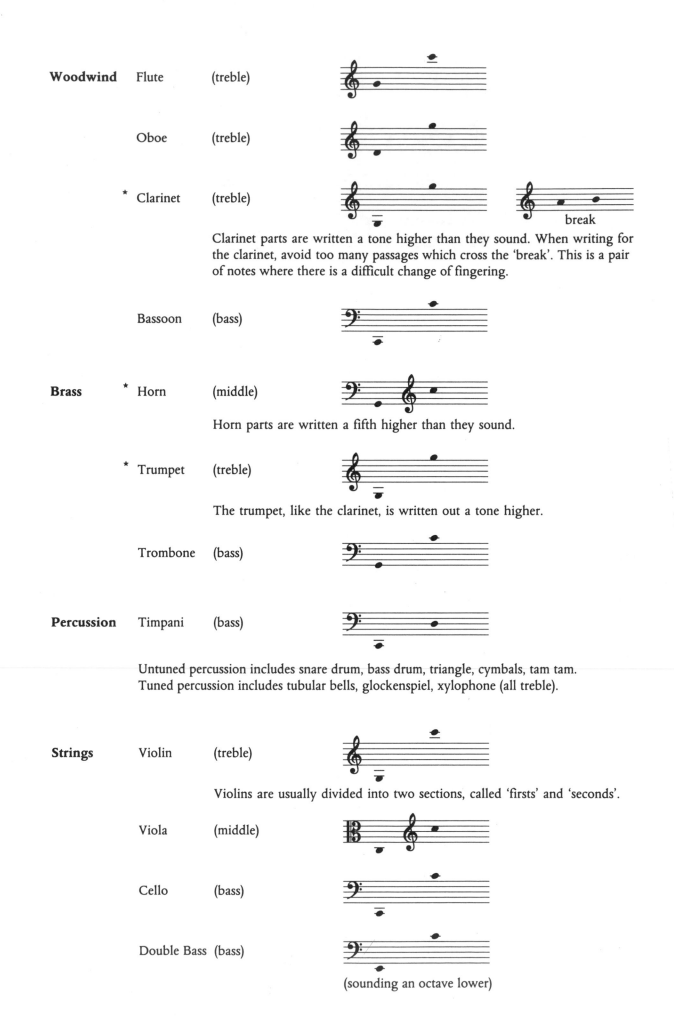

**Woodwind**    Flute    (treble)

Oboe    (treble)

\* Clarinet    (treble)          break

Clarinet parts are written a tone higher than they sound. When writing for the clarinet, avoid too many passages which cross the 'break'. This is a pair of notes where there is a difficult change of fingering.

Bassoon    (bass)

**Brass**    \* Horn    (middle)

Horn parts are written a fifth higher than they sound.

\* Trumpet    (treble)

The trumpet, like the clarinet, is written out a tone higher.

Trombone    (bass)

**Percussion**    Timpani    (bass)

Untuned percussion includes snare drum, bass drum, triangle, cymbals, tam tam.
Tuned percussion includes tubular bells, glockenspiel, xylophone (all treble).

**Strings**    Violin    (treble)

Violins are usually divided into two sections, called 'firsts' and 'seconds'.

Viola    (middle)

Cello    (bass)

Double Bass    (bass)

(sounding an octave lower)

Start with something easy, perhaps a hymn. These are usually written out in **four-part harmony** – that is, the chords are arranged in four-note blocks, two in the upper stave (soprano and alto) and two in the lower stave (tenor and bass).

Jesus, good above all other

Now, write out each of the four parts for a different instrument. For instance:

| Soprano part | Flute |
|---|---|
| Alto part | Violin |
| Tenor part | Clarinet |
| Bass part | Cello |

Try to arrange for instruments which are available in your school, so you get an opportunity to hear your efforts. Each player will need an individual part (see below).

Try experimenting with doublings (see page 41). It may be possible to double the soprano melody part an octave higher or perhaps a third higher (you may need to find a player who can play the higher notes). You could also try doubling the bass part an octave lower.

## Hints on arranging, scoring and copying parts

When writing for wind instruments remember to allow some spaces for breathing.

Each player will need an individual part. There are a number of points to remember when copying out parts.

Make sure a part is properly transposed if the instrument needs this. Get someone to help if in doubt, but try to avoid asking players to transpose their own parts while they play.

If a player has several bars rest, don't write them all out separately. Write one bar, and put the total number of silent bars over the top:

etc.

[53]

Always put bar numbers in the score and in the parts. These are essential in rehearsal, so that players can stop in the middle and find their place easily.

---

### More Ideas

▶ If you are writing a contrapuntal piece, try writing out the parts for a group of instruments.

▶ If you are fitting chords to a melody, try writing out the melody for violin or a woodwind instrument and give the accompaniment to a keyboard. Then try writing out the bass for a bass instrument.

▶ Write a minimalist piece for several instruments to play.

---

# CHAPTER SIX

# Form

Few of the exercises and examples covered so far in this book will result in compositions occupying more than a page of score when written out, or lasting longer than a minute when played, except perhaps the minimalist examples.

A study of **form** will help you build longer pieces. The idea of composing longer pieces may be rather daunting, but if you have already covered the chapters on melody writing and chords, you will be familiar with the techniques of adding ideas together to make musical sections. Most of the principles discussed – for example, the need to balance repetition with variety – apply to form, only on a larger scale.

## Strophic form

This is perhaps the simplest form of all, and consists of a series of repeated verses. Strophic form is typical of the blues, folk songs and hymns, where new words are sung in each verse but to the same melody and chords.

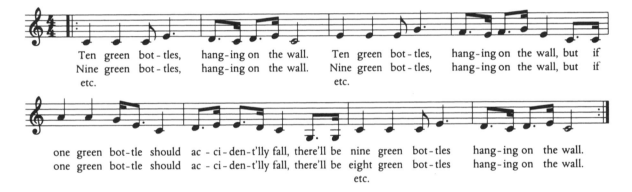

Variety can be introduced in a number of ways. Verses can be played louder or quieter (the final verses of both *Waltzing Matilda* and *Molly Malone* are usually sung quieter as the story of the ghosts is told). It is also possible to vary the tempo.

Even more variety is possible by altering the instrumentation or adding a countermelody or a percussion part.

Songs with choruses are discussed in greater detail in Part IV. However, it is possible to include a chorus within a strophic form. The Christmas carol *The Holly and the Ivy* consists of an alternation of verse and chorus. The melody is the same for both.

ris - ing of the sun _____ and the run - ning of the deer, the _____

play - ing of the mer - ry or - gan, sweet sing - ing in the choir.

Much of what has been said above can be applied to the twelve-bar blues. This is often used as the basic verse structure with the twelve bars repeating over and over. A chorus can be included which, as in *The Holly and the Ivy*, has the same melody as the verses. A recent example of a blues in which this occurs is Prince's *U Got the Look*. It is also common in the blues to include instrumental verses in between the vocal ones.

## Exercises using strophic form

Make an arrangement of a Christmas carol and introduce some variety into the verses. Some could be sung without instrumental accompaniment (called **a capella** singing), and some could incorporate percussion – for example, sleigh bells.

Compose a melody. Write it out four more times so there are five verses in all. Start with the melody on its own, then compose a second part to go with verse 2. Provide another part to go with verse 3, and continue adding new parts to the other verses so they are all different.

## Beginnings, middles and ends – ternary form

One of the simplest forms is **ternary** form. It is also a very satisfying one for the listener because it provides a feeling of setting out on a journey and then returning again, giving a sense of conclusion.

Ternary form is best expressed by the formula ABA. An opening section is followed by a contrasting one, after which the first section is repeated again. A typical example is the **minuet and trio** movement in a classical symphony.

Composing a piece in ternary form is quite easy, in the sense that, having composed the 'A' section, you need only to compose one more section to have all the necessary material for quite a long piece.

In composing the 'B' section it is best to wipe the slate clean, so to speak, and write something completely new to contrast with the first idea, almost as if you were starting again. However, it is important to keep in mind the effect that will be created when the two sections are put together. You need to be clear about the type of contrast you are aiming at.

## Exercises using ternary form

The exercises below all draw on styles and techniques covered in previous chapters.

### 1 Graphics

Chapter 2 described how to write a simple piece based on graphic notation (see page 10). To extend this into a composition in ternary form you will need to compose another section to go in the middle. Alternatively you could decide to use what you've got as the middle section, and compose something to go in front of it. Either way the important thing to decide is what kind of statement you wish to make. Is the new section to be a quiet interlude or a stormy interruption? Or would you prefer the contrast to be more subtle?

Contrast can be achieved in a variety of ways:

▶ Louder or softer

▶ Faster or slower – notes (or patterns) can be closer together or further apart:

fast               slow

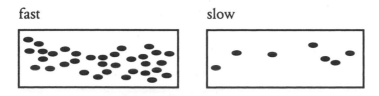

▶ A change of texture could involve fewer or more instruments, or a change of instruments, or a move from smooth to spiky:

smooth           spiky

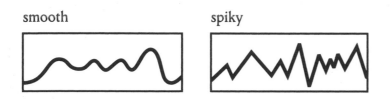

Why not compose the middle section using a completely different technique, perhaps a dice game (see page 13) or proportional notation (see page 12)?

One of the problems with graphic notation is that much of the interpretation is left to the players. Making the graphics in the new section *look* different does not guarantee that the music will *sound* different. As with any composition exercise you have to think of the musical effect you want first. Then find a way of writing it down.

## 2 Minimalism

Because of their reliance on repetition, minimalist pieces can be quite long and tiring for the listener. A middle section may provide relief, especially when the texture is drastically thinned out or when unrelenting pulses and rhythms are interrupted for a while, perhaps by something more sustained.

A middle section may also provide an opportunity to *develop* your ostinati. A development section is an integral part of some forms (see **sonata form**, page 126) and is usually a section where previous ideas are adapted and fresh ones introduced. Ways of introducing variety in minimalist pieces were discussed in the last chapter.

Having worked out how you wish to treat your material you will need to find a way of making the middle section stand out. Here are some suggestions:

▶ Change the instrumentation.

▶ Transpose ideas so they appear one or two octaves higher or lower in the texture, and are therefore more prominent.

▶ Double the idea.

▶ Play it in canon.

▶ Add chords, a drone, accompaniment or backing.

## 3 Melody

Ternary form is particularly suitable for compositions in which melody is a prominent feature. One example is dance movements such as the minuet and trio, where an opening minuet is contrasted with a trio, after which the minuet is repeated. Although some of the principles of contrast discussed in the examples above may feature in the trio section, the main source of contrast is usually a new melody, along with a change of chords or key.

This does not have to be as complicated as it sounds. First, write a simple minuet using techniques discussed in Chapter 3. The minuet is a three-in-a-bar dance; this one is sixteen bars long and is in G major:

Now for the trio. During the Classical period, when it was popular to include a minuet and trio in a symphony, composers customarily wrote the trio in a contrasting key. However, they rarely prepared this new key, or attempted a modulation (see Chapter 10). Instead they jumped straight in, then, at the end, they jumped just as abruptly back into the key of the minuet.

Thus a new and contrasting melody in another key is required. For Classical composers, the choice of key was largely a matter of convention – many composers chose the key of the **tonic minor**. A trio to go with the minuet above would therefore be in G minor.

Minuet D. C. (Minuet *da capo*) is an indication that the minuet is to be repeated to complete the ABA form.

Trios in other related keys are possible. Almost as popular as the tonic minor was the **relative minor**. This is the minor key obtained by playing the notes of the major scale but starting on the sixth degree. Thus the relative minor of G major is E minor; they share the same key signature.

For a minuet in a minor key, the trio was usually in the relative major. This can be found by playing the minor scale but starting on its third degree. Thus the relative major of E minor is G major. A chart of related keys appears in Chapter 10.

A trio in E minor to go with the minuet above might sound like this.

## Song form

Popular songs almost always have a middle section. One basic type of middle section began as a feature of early blues songs and was called the **middle eight** because it was eight bars long. Typically the chords are I, IV and V in a new order, but almost always starting on the subdominant. The progression finishes on the dominant (so as to create an imperfect cadence and lead back to the verse):

There is no specified order for the chords of a middle eight. Here are some variations in the form of a **cue sheet** (see page 73):

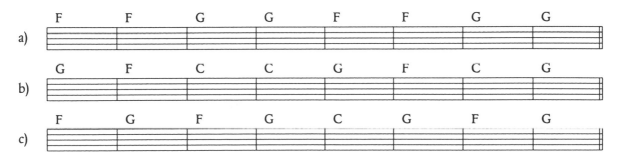

Using a middle eight in conjunction with strophic form, a simple pop song might have the following structure:

Verse 1

Verse 2

Middle eight

Verse 1

This structure is called **song form**. It is broadly ternary, but with the opening verse repeated (AABA). The B section usually starts with a new chord, progressing back to the verse and preparing its re-entry with the dominant.

When writing a middle for a song, remember these points: it does not have to be eight bars long, but try to build your chord progression following the principles of the 'middle eight'. Start with an unexpected new harmony, and conclude the section with the dominant chord so the music leads naturally into the final repeat of the verse.

The concluding bars of a middle section are sometimes called the **turnaround** because they prepare the way for a repeat. Sometimes they constitute a small chord progression in their own right, with the crucial chord, of course, being the dominant:

|  |  |  |  |  |  | turnaround | | |
|---|---|---|---|---|---|---|---|---|
| F | G | F | G | C | G | C | Am | Dm | G |

=== More Ideas ===

► Try composing a pop-type melody in **32-bar song form**. This is a particular type of AABA structure in which the verses and middle section are all eight bars long, adding up to 32 bars.

► Listen to some songs in AABA form. Some typical examples are Buddy Holly (e.g. *Raining in my Heart*) and early Beatles songs (e.g. *Yesterday*).

## Rondo form

The **rondo** is rather like ternary form, but with more than one middle section.

A B C A B A

or A B A C A D A

There is more to composing a rondo than merely writing a few extra sections. These have not only to contrast effectively with the main theme but also with each other. Moreover, the main theme will have to be sufficiently interesting to warrant the additional repeats. You must make the listener want it to come back.

The example opposite is by Couperin (bars at the ends of staves have been split to show the A B A C A form more clearly). Couperin achieves contrast between the sections in two ways. First, much of the melody of the main theme moves in scale patterns whilst the melodies of the B and C sections tend to have more broken chords. Second, the B and C sections are in contrasting keys. Look at the music and see if you can guess what these keys are. Modulation – how to get from one key to another – is discussed in Chapters 9 and 10.

### Exercises using rondo form

Try composing a rondo for two players: a melody part and a bass line. This could be in a pop style using riffs, or it could even be a graphic piece (so long as the main 'theme' is memorable enough). Adopt the structure of the Couperin example. Start with a ternary form (ABA). Then write another section (the C section). Now assemble these – ABACA.

Try working with a group to compose a rondo. Each member of the group composes a melody to make up one of the sections. You could throw a dice to decide who composes the main theme, or you could wait until everyone has finished, listen to all the efforts and decide amongst yourselves which to adopt as the main theme.

[lightly]

## Arch form

This is similar to rondo form, and may have the same number of different sections, but orders them differently:

A  B  C  B  A

or  A  B  C  D  C  B  A

The sections form an overall arch shape. Clearly it is essential to compose each section so that it includes something memorable. This will help your audience to realize, having got past the half-way point, that the piece is repeating in reverse order.

In working with form on this larger scale you will have to learn how to balance one section against another. You may find, as was suggested earlier on, that the section you had intended to be the main one works better as a middle, and that your middle makes a striking main theme. The ability to weigh your ideas and place them effectively takes practice, and you may find it helpful to try several versions of a piece with the sections in different orders.

Listen to some Chopin Waltzes and Scott Joplin Rags. These are well worth studying because they involve the repetition of many contrasting sections and, being written for piano, can be played and easily experimented with in the classroom. Get someone to play them for you. Don't just listen through from start to finish: try starting in the middle to see if any of these later sections *feels* like a main theme. Try copying out the sections, cut your score up and shuffle it on a table top, trying out the piece in different orders.

## Introductions and codas

One problem which many inexperienced composers have is starting and finishing. A piece is easily spoilt if it starts too abruptly or, worse, fizzles out at the end with the players not sure what to do. Like paintings, some pieces need framing.

There are some standard strategies upon which you can draw:

### The 'till ready'

This is common in the theatre where actors need to be given their note – something to walk on to and something to quieten the audience down. It usually takes the form of aa 'oompah' backing, repeated until the singer is ready (hence the name):

Introductions do not have to be this crude though. Many pop songs begin with a type of 'till ready' – a drum introduction or repeated riff.

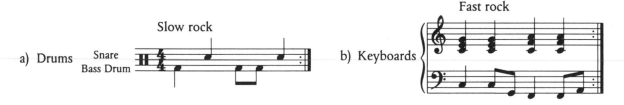

### The fanfare

Other pieces open with a fanfare-type introduction, intended to attract the audience's attention. The ideas in the examples below can be adapted to suit many pieces. It is common to stress the dominant as this creates a feeling of expectation.

[62]

## The mysterious introduction

This is the subtle approach. The audience wonders what is going to happen next. Composers will often use a slow, quiet start to introduce a main theme. Here are two examples of mysterious introductions:

## Codas

Codas achieve the opposite effect to an introduction; they bring the piece to a convincing halt. One common type of coda occurs in a great many pop songs, where a memorable line is repeated over and over at the end, gradually fading out. This type of fade is extremely difficult to reproduce with live performers, although a **rallentando** – a gradual slowing down – will achieve a similar effect.

A coda is often a section in its own right, rather than an effect like a fade or rallentando. It can take a number of forms:

► Repeating the last phrase or the final cadence – this is often played both louder and slower to give it emphasis.

► Thinning out the texture. This could involve instruments dropping out one by one, as in Haydn's 'Farewell' Symphony, or it could involve a sudden change of instrumentation, coupled with slowing down.

► Using an **interrupted cadence** is also effective. This is like a perfect cadence except that the last chord, I, is substituted by something else, usually VI. This tends to leave the cadence (and the listener) in mid-air. Normally a more decisive perfect cadence follows soon after. Here, for example, are the closing bars of a minuet:

► Repeating one of the main ideas over a tonic drone (or pedal) has been a favourite device since the time of Bach. This is the conclusion of his Prelude No. 1 from the *Well-Tempered Clavier*.

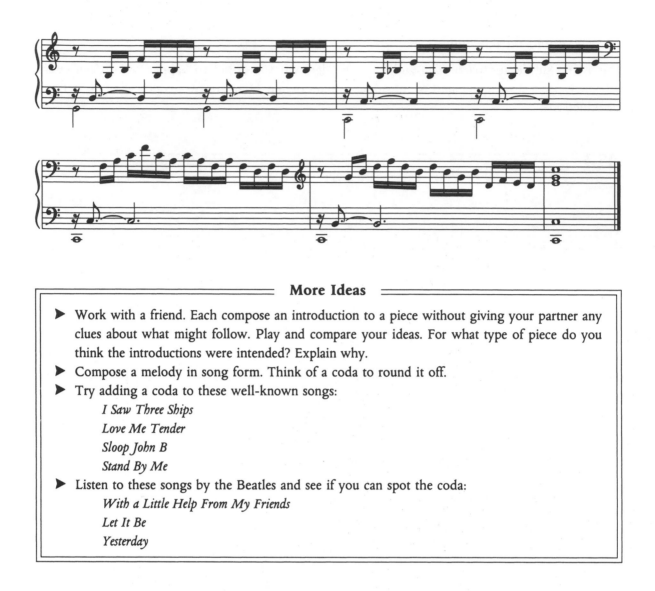

---

### More Ideas

▶ Work with a friend. Each compose an introduction to a piece without giving your partner any clues about what might follow. Play and compare your ideas. For what type of piece do you think the introductions were intended? Explain why.

▶ Compose a melody in song form. Think of a coda to round it off.

▶ Try adding a coda to these well-known songs:

    *I Saw Three Ships*

    *Love Me Tender*

    *Sloop John B*

    *Stand By Me*

▶ Listen to these songs by the Beatles and see if you can spot the coda:

    *With a Little Help From My Friends*

    *Let It Be*

    *Yesterday*

---

## Music for film and TV

Music composed for film and television is a special and interesting case because its form is nearly always determined by the drama and, most important, the visual timing. There is little point in composing a perfect ternary-form piece for a car chase if it does not fit the pictures.

The most commonly heard music on TV or film is the **logo** (the music you hear during the short appearance of a company symbol, e.g. Channel Four, Yorkshire Television or Twentieth Century Fox. Logos usually take the form of a short fanfare.

Title themes are usually complete pieces although they are rarely very long. Each type of programme has its own style. Sport tends to be introduced by marches or rock music, current affairs (including the News) by urgent, repeated rhythms and dramatic fanfares. Drama, especially soap operas, often use strong memorable melodies.

Next time you are watching TV keep a stopwatch close by. Check the timing of some logos and title themes. Try composing a new logo for your local independent TV company.

Listen to a range of title themes and try to identify the features which make them suited to the programme. Then try composing some of your own. Don't worry about length at this stage (some ways of composing music to a set length are described below). Just concentrate on the melody and rhythm, and on getting the general feel right.

Here are some topics and programmes you might try:

> ► A suspense film about a haunted castle
> ► Music to introduce the FA Cup Final
> ► A documentary about factories
> ► A situation comedy set in a hospital

Before you start, consider whether there are any sounds or musical ideas which are associated with the subject and which you could build in. For example, the hospital comedy might feature an ambulance siren or a telephone ringing. The factory programme might feature machine-like rhythms.

*Incidental music*

This is the 'background music' intended to add atmosphere to a drama. It is not supposed to be too obtrusive, although some film directors have deliberately chosen music which is noticeable. One example of this is fast rock music for car chases. Another example, more subtle, is the use of gentle classical music to accompany war scenes, creating an unexpected and shocking contrast.

Most incidental music is composed exactly to match the pictures. This may take the form of **underscoring** a whole scene or part of one, or it may take the form of a **bridge**, a short linking section to join two scenes together.

Suppose, for example, that you are watching someone leave their house and walk happily up the street. The picture then cuts to a pair of feet silently following. You might use skipping rhythms to suggest the happy character, then switch to something tense to accompany the feet, suggesting danger of some sort.

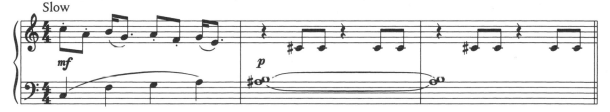

Always avoid thick textures and big dramatic noises. The best film and TV music is very simple, and the secret is always to compose the minimum necessary.

To write music for a sequence of pictures or a dance you will need a stopwatch and a metronome.

1. Watch the scene and decide what sort of music is needed (sometimes the director or performers will tell you what they want). You should have some idea of the musical style and the instruments. There are two ways of calculating the amount of music, depending on the style:

> ► If the music is to consist of sound effects without bar lines you may find it easier not to bother with a time signature and to count in seconds instead.

► If the music has a regular pulse, make a special effort to think of a tempo. Should it be fast, slow, medium? Set your metronome to a tempo which you think might be suitable.

2. Time the scene from start to finish and make a note of the timing.

3. Calculate the number of beats using the following formula:

$$\frac{\text{timing (in seconds)}}{60} \times \text{tempo} = \text{number of beats}$$

Then, to calculate the number of bars, divide by the number of beats per bar (in your chosen time signature). For instance:

$$\text{In } \tfrac{4}{4} \text{ the number of bars} = \frac{\text{number of beats}}{4}$$

$$\text{In } \tfrac{3}{4} \text{ the number of bars} = \frac{\text{number of beats}}{3}$$

4. Sketch out a blank score (or other scoring or cueing system depending upon how you wish to work) with the correct number of empty bars. You may find it useful to make several photocopies so you can try new ideas without having to write out a score each time.

5. With the empty score in front of you, go through the visuals once again marking down any places which you want to bring out in the music (changes of mood, etc.). You will have to watch the visuals again and time all these places; they are called **sync points** – that is, points which must synchronize. You can then use the formula above to calculate the beats on which these points will fall. For instance, for a change of mood after 21 seconds:

$$\frac{21}{60} \times \text{tempo} = \text{place (in beats) where 21 seconds occurs}$$

6. The next stage is a composing one in which you fill in your blank score with music to suit the scenes. You will need to try it out a few times and make any adjustments that are necessary.

---

=== **More Ideas** ===

► Using a stopwatch, time the title theme of a popular quiz show. Compose a new theme for it to exactly the same length.
► Try applying these principles to composing for dance and drama. If there is a dance department in your school compose some music for timed sections of dance. Or compose some background music for a playreading.

---

[66]

# CHAPTER SEVEN

# Trying Out Ideas

The last two chapters in this section are not about studying particular features of music, or composing in particular styles. They are here to help you organize your work and to avoid that awful experience, staring at a blank sheet of paper.

## Where do you start?

Songwriters are often asked this question: 'Do you prefer to start with the tune or with the words?' Many composers count themselves lucky if they know where to start at all. It is because there seem to be so many features to consider – melody, harmony, rhythm, the bass, the accompaniment or backing – that this section begins by looking at the many different ways in which not only songs but compositions in general might be approached.

### Melody

Melodies are amongst the easiest musical structures to compose and perform; they can be sung or tapped out on a keyboard and they are often the most memorable part of a composition.

### The bass line

Some styles and forms are easier to approach if you compose the bass first. This is especially true when the bass has a prominent role, for example in swing jazz (the walking bass), the Baroque textures (the ground bass), Classical music (the Alberti bass), rock 'n' roll and reggae.

### Harmony

In some types of tonal music it is essential to have a clear idea of where the chords are progressing. This may require a chart showing the basic chords so they can be strummed on a guitar, or perhaps an analytical diagram of keys and modulations. It may be helpful to experiment with melody while you listen to the chords playing over; a friend could help with this, or you could record the chords on tape or computer, or use the auto accompaniment available on many electronic keyboards.

### Rhythm

Some songwriters like to work with drum machines – these allow you to select a particular pattern which you can use as a repeated accompaniment while you try out melodies, bass lines and backings.

Rhythm is also a useful way to begin composing melodies or riffs – start by clapping the rhythm and then add the pitches. This process is explained in Chapter 3. In some compositions rhythm can be one of the most important features: examples of this are pieces in uncommon time signatures (5/4 or 7/4) or pieces based on particular dance patterns (waltz, samba, etc.).

### Figurations

If you are composing something which requires an accompaniment it may help if you decide on, and sketch out, the figurations: for example arpeggios, broken chords, block chords, etc.

## Riffs

Riffs are explained in Chapter 3. A great deal of popular music is riff-based. Once you have composed your riff and arranged it for the various backing instruments to your satisfaction then the rest of the song usually follows logically.

## Precomposition

Some pieces are conceived 'at the drawing board'. For example, 12-note rows need to be constructed before composition actually begins; pieces based on chance may need guidelines and rules to be worked out; pieces using graphic notation may require some prior artwork.

## Pencils, paper and pianos

All composers work differently. You may prefer to shut yourself away with a piano, paper and pencil, or perhaps you would rather be with a group of friends around a tape recorder. What is important is that you are able to produce the best results with the least headache.

### Working with an instrument (or the voice)

This is a very common method and usually involves playing and comparing different versions of an idea. The disadvantage of composing with an instrument is that you are limited by your own skill as a performer; you might only ever compose things you are able to play yourself, or you may not have enough hands to play all the ideas at once, especially if you are composing a piece with many parts. Another problem is that the instrument you are using may not be the one you are composing for, and this can be misleading – you may compose something which turns out to be unplayable when it is tried out on the proper instrument.

### Writing and scribbling

Many composers keep sketchbooks. Beethoven's were full of crossings out but he often saved rejected ideas and used them in other pieces. Obviously it is in your interests to be able to write things down in some form or another and to be able to hear what you have written. This makes you independent and not tied to an instrument, but it is not necessary to be able to read full staff notation before you can begin: Chapter 8 describes many different ways of writing music down.

One problem with working on paper is physical; it takes much longer to write down an idea than it does to play it, especially in popular music where the rhythms can be extremely complex. Moreover, scores are arranged in book form so you can only see one or two pages at a time.

### Improvising

Taking a simple idea and elaborating on it in the form of an improvisation can be a useful way of developing a composition, but be careful to record your efforts on tape or you may forget what you did.

### Tape recorders

These are a handy way of saving ideas. One of the most useful pieces of equipment is the four-track recorder (often referred to as a portastudio) because you can get ideas down quickly and mix them together. A technique commonly used in the studio involves recording a **ghost** or **guide track**. This acts as a prompt over which new tracks are recorded, and is discarded at the end. You should be able to record a guide track on a simple cassette recorder if you do not have access to a four track.

*Sequencers*

Some electronic keyboards are equipped with sequencers – the instrument can remember what you have played and will reproduce it for you so you can 'play along with yourself'. The computer sequencer is a much more sophisticated device, although it works along the same lines. The computer will not only allow you to correct mistakes but to add many parts, like a multi-track tape recorder. On some programs you can display the full score, not only printing it out but also copying, deleting and moving entire sections – similar to moving words around on a word processor.

There are three principal ways of composing with computers:

▶ Real time recording – this means using the computer like a tape recorder to remember the details of your performance.

▶ Cycle recording – here the computer runs like a drum machine. That is, it keeps repeating the same one or two bars from the beginning. You will have to decide before you start how many bars you want repeated and then make this setting on the computer. Then, with the computer in recording mode, you play the piano keyboard. Each time the computer goes back to the start it will remember and repeat anything you played during the previous repeat. It is therefore possible to build up a complicated melody or drum part bit by bit without stopping the recording.

▶ Step time – the computer does not 'run' like a tape recorder. Instead you 'type' in the melody either by playing it on the keyboard or by writing it onto the screen as if on a sheet of paper. The computer organizes the resulting 'list' of musical events into beats and bars.

Technology has made music more accessible than it has ever been before, but it is not without disadvantages. The need to stare at the computer screen, headphones firmly clamped on to shut out the world, can tend to turn the creation of music into a solitary activity. Also, the computer is almost always used in conjunction with a piano-type keyboard. It is extremely difficult to combine computers with acoustic orchestral instruments unless you have a great deal of money, and although there are ways of connecting electronic string and wind instruments these never seem to be as popular either with players or composers.

*Working in groups*

Working as part of a group is commonplace in pop, jazz and in many other cultures. Two types of music where it works best are pop, when everyone has a definite role to play – for example a drummer, bass player, rhythm section and so on – and in minimalist-type pieces (see Chapter 5) where the players all make an equal contribution.

## Fitting the piece together

One of the hardest things for a composer to do is to imagine what the final piece will be like, or to imagine sections which haven't been played or written out yet.

What can be most helpful in any composition is some kind of outline, so you are able to keep the end of the piece in sight and monitor where you are going. This could take the form of a diagram or a list.

It may help to write out a blank score and fill it in bit by bit. For example, if you know that a melody you are writing will be sixteen bars long you could lay out all sixteen bars, filling in the bits you can and leaving the rest until later.

Because music is an art form which exists in time it is tempting to think it is always composed by starting at the beginning and continuing to slog away until you get to the last bar. In fact there are several ways of fitting a piece together.

### Starting with the details (the house building method)

You have a picture in your head of the final structure and proceed to build it, brick by brick. In musical terms this may mean starting at bar 1 and working steadily through to the end; or it may involve composing motifs, then building them into phrases, then building the phrases into sections and so on.

### Starting with the structure

This might be called the landscape gardening method: the big items like lawns and paths are put in first and the details filled in at the end. You might adopt this method when composing a sonata by writing all the tunes first, or if you are working on a piece of counterpoint you could start by sketching in all the entries. Jazz compositions, in which the choruses are written out and the intervening solos filled in later, are sometimes composed using this approach.

### Editing

This is similar to film-making. You compose all the sections you need to make up the piece but do not, at this stage, attempt to fit them together. When all the composing is complete the sections are joined up in the same way that a film editor joins all the bits of a film. This method works well in song writing, where the sections are all very clearly defined (verse, chorus, middle) and where several different running orders may be possible. It is also helpful when you have had a good idea but cannot decide where in the piece to use it.

### Layering

Building up a composition part by part is almost standard practice in the recording studio, particularly with pop music. Usually the drums are recorded first, then the bass is added, then the rhythm parts and so on until the lead vocals finish it off. This is also a useful way of composing counterpoint because it forces you to write flowing, independent parts.

### Using prompts

The use of ghost tracks has already been discussed (see page 68): a version of the piece is recorded, perhaps on guitar, and this serves as a guide to which other parts are added, but which is itself discarded at the end. Such a process is also possible using 'ghost' ostinati or accompaniment figures which you can use to get going but which do not feature in the final composition.

### Composing backwards

Not literally backwards, of course. Imagine you are writing the middle section of a song, or the transition of a sonata for which it is necessary to plan a move from one key to another. You will find it much easier if you start at the destination and then retrace your steps, working out in stages what harmonies will be necessary. Also, if you are writing a piece which involves transformation of a phrase or melody (for example, music in a minimalist style) you could compose the final section first and then work out what you need to compose in order to relate it to the opening.

## Stuck for ideas

There are occasions when your imagination is fired and when the conditions are right for getting ideas down quickly. More likely, however, you will be plagued by interruptions and indecision. Or you fall prey to any one of a number of common problems:

▶ You have a good idea – only to forget it before you have the chance of trying it out at the piano.
*Solution*: Behave as if you had lost something, like your keys. Try not to panic, and retrace your steps.

▶ You like your idea but someone else says they don't, and this puts you off.
*Solution*: Don't listen to comments until the piece is finished or performed, unless the comments are from someone you trust.

▶ Your idea sounds like something else you have heard.
*Solution*: Try to be honest with yourself. Have you been influenced by something and, if so, by how much? If you are not able to identify the source, try to pinpoint exactly what it is that sounds familiar by a process of elimination. Is it the melody? If so, which bit? Or is it the chords? Or the drum pattern?

▶ You don't like your idea.
*Solution*: In this case there is not much to do but start again. However, try to decide first if your dislike is rational. Is there really something wrong with the piece? Or is it the way you are playing it? Are you perhaps feeling shy about people hearing it? In this case you may just need to do a little more work before you are ready to share it with others.

▶ You have got so far and run out of ideas.
*Solution 1*: Put away the thing you were working on and imagine you are starting all over again. In this way you might come up with a new section.
*Solution 2*: Take what you consider to be the most interesting bar or phrase and write three variations. Choose the best of these and use it to start a new section.

# CHAPTER EIGHT

# Reading and Writing

The question of how compositions should be written out and, indeed, whether it is necessary for them to be written out at all, has been much debated in recent years.

Some musicans believe that you are not properly trained unless you can read and write staff notation. This may be true for some styles of music – but not necessarily pop and jazz which are usually played by ear involving a large element of improvisation and which tend to be recorded rather than written down. The argument is further complicated when technology is used in composing, since some computers can print scores even if the operator cannot read a note.

The extent to which these issues matter depends upon how you define reading, playing and composing. Nevertheless most people would agree that one of the composer's main tasks is to find a way of communicating the details of a composition as accurately as possible so that it can be rehearsed and performed with a minimum of fuss.

There are three principal ways of achieving this: systems based on staff notation, systems based on proportional or graphic notation, and systems based on technology.

## Staff notation

This is the conventional system of reading and writing music using the five-line staff, and will be familiar to most people learning the piano or an orchestral instrument.

Although it is very common it has its drawbacks. First, it is quite complicated and can take a long time to learn; in fact many people have discovered while learning an instrument that they tend to play more fluently when they ignore the score. Second, staff notation is notoriously bad at communicating subtlety. For example there is no precise or accepted system for telling a clarinet player how hard to blow and therefore how harsh or soft the tone of the instrument should be. Similarly there is no clear way of notating small variations of rhythm and pulse – what we might call the 'feel' of the performance. Imagine a song, sung first by an opera singer, then by a jazz singer. The differences between the two performances would be strikingly obvious yet very difficult indeed to notate.

The full orchestral score involves music written on many staves, because each instrument has its own line. Music copied out in this way can look very professional but requires a fair degree of writing skill and confidence. Beginners are advised to adopt something simpler.

A great deal of time can be saved by sketching your work (or even making a final copy) either on a single staff:

or on treble and bass staves as if for piano (such a score is sometimes called a 'piano reduction' or 'short score'):

If two staves are not sufficient you could extend them by adding a third (an extra treble or an extra bass) and even a fourth (as if for piano duet).

A three-line stave is perfectly adequate for much percussion music and is easier to read:

Composers of pop, jazz and show music are inclined to use simplified versions of the score. Performers may be given music to play in the form of a **cue sheet** (sometimes called a **chord chart**). This is like a blank part giving only the basic information, for example bar lines, repeat marks, chord symbols and important cues. (Chord symbols are explained in Chapter 5). The performer would be expected to use the cue sheet as a guide while they improvise their part.

There are several circumstances when cue sheets can be useful: when some of the players (or you the composer) are not fluent readers, when there is a large element of improvisation, when the piece or its style is sufficiently well known to the players not to need the details spelling out, or when the music is so rhythmically complex that it would either be unreadable or unwriteable. It is for this latter reason that guitar parts are almost never copied out exactly as they are to be played – the page would be black with notes.

The **lead sheet** is similar to the cue sheet but here the player is given the vocal part with words and possibly chords. This enables players to follow the words, even if they cannot read the notes.

Sometimes rock bands simplify the cue sheet even further: the staff is abandoned completely, and all the players are given is a list of chords:

```
A   A   G   G
A   A   G   G
A   D   A   E
A   C   D   G
```

Very often the players will simply play the chords from memory after agreeing a basic structure. This is sometimes referred to as a **head arrangement**.

The usual format for publishing a popular song is in song-sheet form, and this consists of an arrangement for piano with the vocal line above. It is very unusual for this type of music ever to appear in full score, although it is becoming more common. When an arrangement uses a lot of orchestral instruments the composer or arranger will often compose directly into the individual parts – but take care, this requires experience.

## Graphic and proportional notation

Systems based upon pictures, diagrams and graphs became very popular with composers in the post-war avant-garde movement, and arose for a variety of reasons. First, the scope of instrumental playing was advancing very quickly and a wide range of new techniques required notations to be invented for them. Second, composers found the five-line staff too limiting for the reasons discussed above. Last, and perhaps most important, composers wished to explore the potential of scores using colour, patterns, diagrams and pictures. Usually this was done in pieces which involved an element of chance; the graphics allowed the players a very wide range of interpretation.

### Graphic notation

As you will have seen in Chapter 2, graphics can be employed to suggest the feel, rather than the details, of an improvised passage of music. However, you may find it helpful to find ways of making the symbols more accurate. In the following examples the amount of detail is gradually increased to demonstrate how graphics might be developed towards an understanding of staff notation.

As a first stage the symbols take the form of dots like primitive note-heads to suggest short, fast-moving phrases:

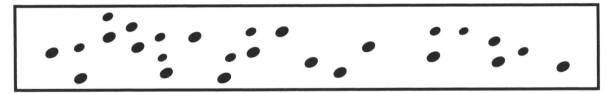

These scattered patterns can further be refined so as to specify the melodic shape of the phrases:

If the note heads in the example above are drawn onto a staff, you can indicate which intervals you want:

In the course of one more step we might introduce note values and rhythm:

*Proportional notation*

This is a way of notating music without the precision of conventional note values and rests. It tends to be employed in the notation of free-moving music which has no clear pulse or rhythmic feel. Usually the score is divided up into sections with signs to be cued by a conductor or marked off in seconds (see Chapter 2).

One very simple method is to write out the note names in line and in the order in which they are to be played.

**C  C  G  G  A  B  C  A  G**

Obviously the score gives no clue about rhythm or metre. Up to a point these features can be incorporated by writing the note names on squared paper, with each square representing a beat.

| C |  | C |  | G |  | G |  | A | B | C | A | G |  |  |  |

In most proportional scores the duration of notes is indicated by lines; the shorter the line, the shorter the note.

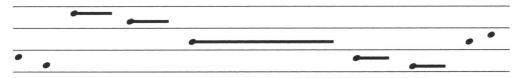

Additional symbols may have to be devised to accommodate the characteristics of particular instruments. For example, xylophones cannot sustain notes unless a tremolo is indicated, perhaps by a wavy line. You may also need to devise a simple way of indicating pitch. In the example below the notes are arranged in three bands: high notes in the top band, middle notes in the middle and low ones at the bottom.

A final word of caution. Graphic and proportionally notated scores can be attractive to work with and to look at. The danger is allowing yourself to get sidetracked, producing beautiful scores and uninteresting music.

## Technology-based systems

The scope of technology is now so great that for many musicians it has replaced the need to read or write. The tape recorder and computer are the notepads of the future, allowing you to record on cassette, print scores at the push of a button or store the details of performances on computer disk. You could argue that over-reliance upon machines is 'cheating', although there can be little doubt that a computer which is able to carry out repetitive and time-consuming operations like copying, transposing and making parts is a godsend.

An increasing number of musicians, particularly in the pop and jazz fields, are relying upon technology to print out scores, even though they cannot read themselves. A number of alternative notations have grown up.

*Drum patterns*

There is very often a section devoted to these in music technology magazines so that enthusiasts can write in with their favourite drum patterns. Most are based on the grid-like display seen on drum machines: the grid usually represents one bar, divided into sixteen semiquavers. A dot is written on each semiquaver beat where a particular part of the drum kit is to play. Having programmed this pattern into the machine it will then repeat it.

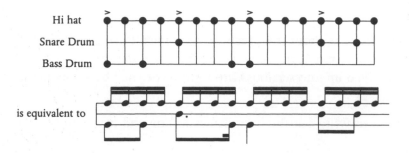

Computers are usually able to display music in a grid form of this sort, as an alternative to staff notation.

## Track sheets

This is effectively a cue sheet which tells the recording engineer which instruments and parts are recorded on which tracks of a multi-track recorder.

|  | Verse | | Chorus | Middle |
|---|---|---|---|---|
| **Track 1** | Guitar | | | |
| **Track 2** | | Drums | | |
| **Track 3** | | Bass | | |
| **Track 4** | | | Keyboards | |
| **Track 5** | | | Saxophone | (solo) |

## Event displays

These are usually available as a display feature of sequencers. Sequencers are explained in Chapter 15. An event display provides a method of recording pitch and rhythm (and other performance information) using letters and numbers. It would be very laborious to compose an entire piece using events, but they can be a helpful way of notating short, repeated patterns such as drums and percussion, bass riffs and ostinati.

Each note is identified using three numbers, which together show its position in the song, plus a letter to denote pitch and a further number to denote which octave. The first number indicates the bar, the second indicates the beat, the third indicates a subdivision of the beat, e.g. semiquaver or triplet. Thus **1 1 1 C4** means Middle C (on most keyboards and sequencers), to be played on the first semiquaver of the first beat of the first bar.

Here is an example of a bass riff, first of all written in staff notation:

It would appear like this in an event display:

```
1   1   1   D3
1   2   3   D3
1   3   1   C3
1   3   3   A2
1   4   1   C3
2   1   1   D3
2   4   1   D3
```

## Voice data charts

The instruction manual which comes with keyboard synthesizers sometimes contains a very useful table which can be photocopied. This identifies the various buttons and programming functions so that, if you alter the quality of a sound in some way, you can use the table to record what you did. It should be quite easy to make a table of your own, based on what you know about your equipment, and to use this as a simple method of 'scoring' timbre.

## Graphics and word processing

Some computer programs allow you to produce very elaborate designs suitable for graphic scores. The possibilites of scores consisting of words is explored in Chapter 2. Writing and printing pieces based on words would be very easy using a word processing program.

# Part III
## Style Studies

Parts I and II were concerned with basic skills. Now you will learn how to apply some of those skills to the composition of style studies in pastiche modal and tonal music. This involves learning the harmonic and contrapuntal techniques associated with different historical styles, and often leads students to ask, 'Why would anyone want to imitate the sounds of history?' There are several answers:

▶ It will help you to read and write music more fluently

▶ One way of learning how music works is to try to compose it

▶ Some techniques are easier learnt in their original style

▶ Familiarity with different types of musical grammar will strengthen your technique
   as a composer

▶ It is a compulsory part of many examinations

Obviously there is not space to study the individual characteristics of every composer. Instead, four periods have been selected for study in a step-by-step way:

The late Renaissance (*c.* 1550–1600)

The late Baroque (*c.* 1700–1750)

The Classical period (*c.* 1750–1800)

The early Romantic period (*c.* 1800–1850)

The steps involve the composition of melody, counterpoint and textures, and the study of harmony and form.

# CHAPTER NINE

# Melody

## The late Renaissance

The Renaissance was enormously rich in musical style and invention. The period from 1550 to 1600 saw the beginnings of opera, a huge growth in home music-making in the form of the madrigal, and the development of specialized compositions for instruments.

Some examples of early instrumental composition will be covered later. This section starts with the melody of sacred vocal music, as exemplified in the music of Palestrina.

Palestrina is often regarded as the master of sixteenth-century vocal polyphony, and his melodies have a timeless, peaceful quality. They derive this from **plainsong**, to which they are related. You may find it helpful to try composing some imitation plainsong, even though, being a medieval style, it falls outside the dates we set above.

Plainsong was a form of sacred vocal music. It is usually written without indicating the rhythm; the words themselves provide this framework, producing a sort of speech-song with no definite pulse. Note how some of the vowels are prolonged. This type of phrase is called a **melisma**.

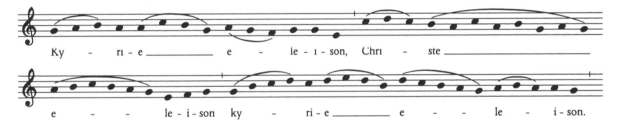

Latin was the common liturgical language (even though the example above is in Greek), but if you find this a little forbidding try picking a passage in English out of the Bible and setting that instead. Try to stick to the following musical guidelines:

▶ Keep the range of the plainsong within an octave

▶ Move in conjunct motion (especially during the melismata) and use leaps sparingly

▶ Avoid leaps greater than a fifth

▶ If you do include a leap try to approach and leave it from 'inside' the interval, thus:

Once you have mastered this, try composing a melody with the rhythm written out. At all costs avoid strong, snappy rhythms like these, because they will suggest an unauthentic two- or four-bar pattern:

Instead, note values should be irregular and follow the words. The example below, and later ones in this chapter, are written out in 4/4 time. However, you may find editions of sixteenth-century music written in 4/2. Concentrate on composing a flowing melody which follows the general principles of plainsong. Once you are confident with this you are only a short step from the next stage – adding parts to make counterpoint (see pages 100–103). Here is a simple setting of part of the Lord's Prayer:

Our      Fa  -  ther  who  art      in _____  hea  -  ven

Don't be afraid to tie notes over the bar line. Tied notes will be studied in more detail in the chapter on harmony (see page 89).

Our      Fa  -  ther _____  who  art  in  hea  -  ven _____

(see pages 100–103)

## Exercises

Compose a setting of the word 'Amen' in which the note values are all written out. Extend the 'A-' syllable with a melisma (but don't go on for ever or there will not be spaces for the singers to take a breath).

Next, try a setting of a psalm.

## The late Baroque

Baroque melody is often described as florid. Like the painting and architecture of the period it tends to be decorative; the intricate detail, and the way the phrases are often quite long and drawn out, can make melodies tricky to compose. The rhythms, on the other hand, tend to be more straightforward than in Renaissance vocal music, often being based on dances.

To start with, experiment with simple ideas. Write a short melody of crotchets and quavers.

Now decorate this with figurations. Here are some examples of how the first two notes might be decorated:

The original melody might be finished off like this – taking care not to overdo the semiquavers:

Once you have mastered some features of this florid style you can try building longer melodies, using the techniques learnt in Chapter 3. One way to extend a melody is to build a sequence. Here we will compose a sequential answering melody to go with the one above. Get the basic phrase right first, then try it out starting on different notes. Descending sequences are usually easier than ascending ones, but you may have to experiment for a while until it sounds right. If you think there is a danger of losing your sense of direction you might try sketching out the harmony first – but keep it simple.

Now try putting the melody together. In the example below we have a simple ABA structure.

The figurations used in the cadence have a marked effect upon whether or not the melody sounds Baroque in style. Here are a few more examples – and you can find still more by looking at the closing bars of the Two-Part Inventions by Bach:

Repetition was an important feature of Baroque melody, particularly in all forms of instrumental music. In the example below – from Vivaldi's set of concerti *The Four Seasons* (Concerto No. 3, *Autumn*, first movement) – the melody is repeatedly thrown back and forth between the full orchestra and the solo violin.

Clearly, it is possible to extend melody quite considerably by using this combination of repetition and instrumental contrast. Many composers developed this to provide a sense of dialogue. Melodic structure is based on the characteristics of dramatic speech, and is composed so as to suggest questions, answers and changes of expression. The example below is constructed in this manner, like a conversation.

First we compose an outline for the opening phrase.

Now the decorations are added.

You can use the same process to compose an answering phrase.

Then add a sequence (see Chapter 3).

You can add even more to your melody by adopting a device popular amongst Baroque composers: composing new phrases to follow the final cadence so the melody has the feeling of being interrupted and extended. Here is the complete melody with its extended ending:

Write out the first four bars of a melody by Bach or Handel. Try composing a phrase to answer it. Keep the rhythm flowing.

Copy out the rhythm of a Baroque melody. Now try to construct a new melody by adding your own notes to the rhythm you have copied out.

## The Classical period

Beginners tend to find Classical melody easier to compose than the melody of other periods. This is because its proportions were based on four-bar phrases and repetition of ideas – the principles we explored in Part I, in fact. Particularly important was repetition of rhythm. Here we will use techniques discussed in Part I to 'compose' a melody by Mozart (from the String Quartet K458, nicknamed 'The Hunt'). The melody is from the last movement, a typically unfussy finale theme with an ABAB structure.

Start by clapping two different rhythms:

Then add the notes:

Extending Classical melody further is not quite so simple, however. A major feature of the style was contrast of key. You will have to look up harmony in Chapter 10, particularly the section on modulation, before you can explore Classical melody much further.

It is possible, though, to grasp some of the basics of modulation by studying melody. The theme in the example below is by Haydn (from the finale of his Symphony No. 99) and is, like the Mozart, based on a repeated rhythm. What is different is that this one finishes by modulating to the dominant – typically the first port of call in a classical piece. See how Haydn makes this possible by introducing the A natural (the all-important leading note of the dominant):

Now the Mozart melody above will be changed by introducing a modulation to the dominant (F). This means the introduction of the leading note of F major (E natural). As in the example by Haydn this will be left until the very last minute:

Another important feature of Classical melody was extremes of contrast from bar to bar, especially during first movements. Here is an example of an opening theme from the first movement of a sonata. The harmonies are very basic and it is constructed as follows:

Bars 1–2 Two-bar fanfare-like call to attention
Bars 3–4 Two-bar answer – more lyrical and finishing with an imperfect cadence
Bars 5–8 The rhythm of the first four bars is repeated with dominant harmony, leading back to the tonic with a perfect cadence
Bars 9–20 A new idea based on the rhythm of the opening and leading to a sequence

At this point the example is 20 bars into what might well be a sonata. To find out how and where to go from here, turn to pages 126–132.

## Exercises

Invent a one-bar rhythm. Now compose an eight-bar melody based on that rhythm. When you have done that add a further eight bars, modulating to the dominant at the end.

Two favourite opening gestures amongst Classical composers were the *coup d'archet* and the 'Mannheim sky rocket'. The *coup d'archet* was a flashy and difficult-to-play opening phrase for the strings. This one is from Beethoven's Second Symphony.

The Mannheim sky rocket is an ascending arpeggio, so called because it was a favourite effect amongst composers in eighteenth-century Mannheim (although the term itself is a modern-day one). This rocket (or, rather, pair of rockets) is also from Beethoven: the Piano Sonata Opus 2 No. 1.

Try composing a Classical melody incorporating one of these devices. They work best when contrasted with something gentle and lyrical. Try to maintain the feeling of drama and change.

[84]

## The Romantic period

One of the features of music in the Romantic period was increasingly complex and chromatic harmony. This developed throughout the nineteenth century alongside compositions which made increasing demands upon the virtuoso skills of the player. Clearly, the novice composer will find the styles of, for example, Chopin or Brahms very difficult. Yet the fact that pages of music by these composers are black with notes does not necessarily mean there is 'more' music. In many instances it is simply a case of the figurations being much more elaborate. Perhaps the best way to approach Romantic melody is to experiment with non-essential chromatic notes.

The example below is from a Chopin Waltz (Opus 69 No. 1 in A flat major). For ease of study it has been transposed into C.

Note the chromatic notes and the wide melodic leaps. The basic structure, however, might be written out as follows:

## Exercises

Write a simple melodic outline.

Then fill it in with chromatic passing notes and auxiliaries. Make sure they fall on a weak beat – that way you can devise a melody with simple harmony and still employ chromatic notes.

Most virtuoso writing consists of scalic runs, arpeggios and sequences. Have a look at some of the piano studies by Czerny and the *Études* (also meaning 'studies') by Chopin. In most cases the harmonies are actually quite simple although the figurations are very complex.

# CHAPTER TEN

# Harmony

One of the reasons why Classical music and popular music sound so different from each other is that each style conforms to a different set of guidelines. For example, the following chord progression is quite common in popular music:

However, a succession of parallel triads such as these would be unusual in classical music (although for every 'rule' like this it is possible to find an example of its being broken).

This chapter is about guidelines for traditional harmony and counterpoint. Certain sounds and progressions are generally taken to be 'forbidden' in most tonal and modal music from the Renaissance onwards; these might therefore be regarded as 'ground-rules' upon which to base a study of harmony.

## *Consecutive fifths and octaves*

These occur when two parts move in similar motion a fifth or octave apart.

Consecutive fifths are likely to occur when you are progressing between chords whose roots are a second apart – for example, IV to V.

## *Exposed fifths and octaves*

These occur when the outer parts jump in the same direction and land on a fifth or octave.

## Exercises in three- and four-part harmony

In Chapter 4 there is an exercise which involves choosing a chord progression and then writing it out in three separate parts (melody, bass and an inner part). One of the secrets of a smooth progression is good **voice leading**. There is more to harmony than chords placed next to one another like books being stacked on a shelf. You have to pay attention to the movement of each part. As a general rule try to write parts which are singable.

The example below shows a melody harmonized in three parts. There is  considerable scope for improvement. For example, the bass part jumps from the leading note in bar 2 down to the tonic in bar 3. It would have been much smoother to sing if it had moved *up* (which is the direction the ear would expect it to go). Also, some of the chords have important notes, such as the third, missing.

When reworked the parts are much more vocal and smooth:

One of the exercises in Chapter 5 involves arranging the four parts of a hymn for four different instruments. Try writing out a hymn in four parts and see if you can work out what the chords are and which notes of the chord are in which part. This hymn-type four-part texture is sometimes called an SATB arrangement – which stands for the four vocal parts: soprano, alto, tenor, bass.

Obviously a three-note chord will have one of its notes duplicated in a four-part texture. This provides an element of choice which some feel makes four-part harmony easier than three-part. Some textbooks recommend that you avoid doubling the third of a major chord if possible, but as you will see in the example below, Bach feels able to ignore this rule.

The example below is part of a Bach chorale. Chorales were hymn tunes, developed by Martin Luther during the 1520s. There are hundreds of versions harmonized by Bach.

Was Gott tut, das ist wohlgetan

These four-part Bach chorales are often used in harmony exams – you would normally be given a chorale with parts missing which you would be required to fill in.

Try completing some Bach chorales with a friend. Each write out a chorale for the other with a part missing. To begin with miss out an inner part as this makes an easier exercise. You should also try the **figured bass** exercises on pages 90–91.

## Dissonance

A dissonant note is one which does not belong to the notes of a triad. Some 'foreign' notes clash more than others and it is the composer's ability to manipulate these clashes which adds spice to a progression of chords.

There are certain rules involved in using dissonance, but they are based on simple principles. Chord changes normally occur on a strong beat. At this point the notes of the chord should be consonant with the bass. Consonant intervals are the third, fifth and octave. The sixth is also allowed in the case of a first inversion chord.

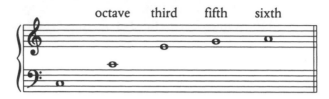

All other intervals – 2nds, 4ths and 7ths – are considered dissonant and, when you wish to use them for effect, they must be introduced and resolved in a particular way.

The simplest instance is the **accented passing note** in which there are three stages to the process:

1   The dissonance is approached from the note above or below
2   It clashes on the strong beat
3   It resolves onto a consonance on the next weak beat

In the example below the dissonance is a fourth, resolving onto the third below:

Similar to the accented passing note is the **appoggiatura**. The difference is that the melody leaps to the dissonance instead of approaching it by step.

In this example the dissonance is a seventh, resolving onto the sixth:

Slightly more sophisticated is the **suspension**. Here, the dissonant note is prepared in the preceding chord, 'held over' the strong beat, and resolved onto the next weak beat.

The **struck suspension** is somewhere between a suspension and an accented passing note. Composers sometimes join several struck suspensions together to form a sequence.

Dissonances of more than one note are possible. In the final cadence of many Classical compositions the dominant chord is often suspended, creating an effect that is almost a cliche. In the example below, note also the struck suspension in bar 1, 3rd beat. The octaves in the left hand are not consecutives – they are 'allowed' as a piano-writing device.

### The second inversion chord

This includes a note which is a fourth above the bass so it is, by its nature, a dissonant chord. Apart from Renaissance counterpoint, in which it is avoided, there are a number of circumstances when its use is allowed.

One is known as the **passing six-four** ('six-four' because these are the intervals from the bass note to the other two notes of the triad). In the passing six-four the bass itself is a passing note.

Another very common use of the second inversion chord is the **cadential six-four**. This is really a glorified suspension.

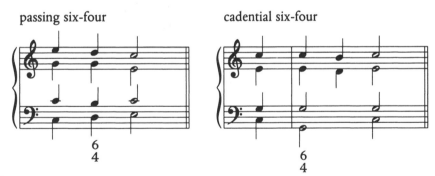

passing six-four                    cadential six-four

# Figured bass

One special type of bass line, in extensive use throughout the Baroque, was the **figured bass**. It involved a bass instrument (usually a cello) playing the written part and a harpsichord filling in chords above it. The chords were specified in the form of numbers written beneath the bass line, and it was then left to the harpsichord player to work out – and choose, within the contraints of the figured bass – exactly what to play. (See also *continuo* in the next chapter.)

Corelli: Sonata da Chiesa, Opus 1 No.10

The figures are a form of shorthand and indicate the position, by its interval above the bass, of the most important note in the chord.

No figures at all indicate a chord in root position (root in the bass, plus fifth and third above)

6 is a first inversion (the root is a sixth above the bass)

$\frac{6}{4}$ is a second inversion

$\frac{6}{5}$, $\frac{4}{3}$ and $\frac{4}{2}$ are all inversions of the seventh chord

sharps and flats indicate chromatic alteration to the third of the chord, or
to others notes if indicated

Although it may seem impossibly complicated at first, continuo players can follow the figures with as much imagination and as little effort as a rock guitarist following a chord chart.

## Four-part exercises using figured bass

The figured bass is sometimes set in music exams. It can take the form of a chorale in which you will be given the soprano and bass part (along with the figures) and be asked to fill in the two missing inner parts in accordance with those figures.

Brunquell aller Güter

A much harder exercise involves starting with the bass alone and having to compose a melodic soprano part on top. In these cases it is best to write the melody first, choosing notes from the implied chords. To do this, write the chords out above the bass – since this is for reference only there is no need to worry about good part writing. Then trace a melody, remembering to leave space for the two inner parts.

[90]

Now complete the inner parts. You may have to make a few adjustments, even perhaps compromising the soprano melody slightly, in order to fit the four parts together. Don't forget to check all the parts thoroughly for consecutives! You need to make six checks:

## Seventh chords

A triad is made up of three notes, each a third apart – root, third, fifth. If another note is added a third above the fifth, a new type of chord is created, a seventh.

Seventh chords are a common feature of popular music and jazz (and are discussed in Part V). However, their use in these styles is slightly freer than in 'classical' harmony, which is the subject of this chapter.

The seventh is generally treated as a dissonance. In other words it has usually to be resolved, or at least a resolution implied. The most common seventh is the **dominant seventh**, a very powerful chord to use in a perfect cadence because it contains the interval of a diminished fifth:

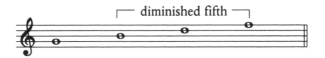

This interval, particularly when it is part of a dominant seventh, tends to pull very strongly to resolve onto the tonic and its third, either inwards or outwards depending on the voicing:

The seventh itself is usually prepared as part of chord II or chord IV, the entire cadence being:

Any chord can have a seventh added, and sevenths are particularly effective when they form a sequence. Note how this bass falls in regular fifths:

## Modulation

Modulation, the technique of moving from one key to another, was touched upon in the last chapter. Chapter 6 also showed how some forms are based on contrast of keys.

A new key is normally introduced by its dominant, and some chromatic alteration of the scale is usually needed to make this possible. In the following example by Clementi there is a modulation in bars 7 and 8. Clementi achieves this by constructing a perfect cadence in the new key. This is clearly signposted by the alteration of C to C sharp (the new leading note).

He also introduces a subtle change in the harmony of the second phrase in order to make the modulation smoother. In bar 6 he moves to E minor, which serves as a pivot; this chord is VI in G and II in D. Note the cadential six-four chord in bar 7.

D is, of course, the dominant of G, and the dominant is the key to which composers most frequently modulate, especially in the course of a four- or eight-bar phrase structure.

Another common destination is the relative minor. Here, bars 5–8 of the Clementi example are re-written so that the phrase ends in E minor. This is done in three stages:

1  Plan the chords:

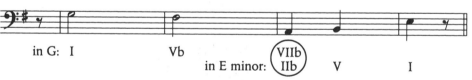

2  Articulate the chords with figurations to match the opening phrase:

3  Devise a melody whose rhythm matches that of the opening phrase:

For a piece that starts in a minor key, the most common modulation will be to the relative major.

Choose a key and devise a set of chords modulating to the dominant. Devise another set modulating to the relative minor (if in a major key) or the relative major (if in a minor key). Try some experiments to see how *few* chords are needed for a convincing modulation.

Study some Baroque and Classical pieces, for example dance suites or minuets and trios, and identify the modulations.

Try writing out the first sixteen bars of a modulating melody and see if you can rewrite the

Find a piece which modulates and make a note of the chord progressions used in the modulation. Write these chords out and compose a new melody over the top. Try composing a completely new piece based on these chord progressions.

*Problematic modulations*

Beware of modulations to the subdominant. In some forms, for example some of those discussed in Chapter 6, it is possible when starting a new and contrasting section to jump into a different key and out again at the end without preparation. Whilst this can be done with the subdominant, there are some circumstances where a modulation to the subdominant can have a feeling of permanence and it can be very difficult indeed to get back again.

A modulation to the subdominant involves a chromatic alteration to the leading note by flattening it. Loss of the leading note considerably weakens your chances of returning to the home key with a feeling of finality.

In the above example the melody modulates to the subdominant and then back to the tonic. However, the last bar sounds far from final.

The ease or difficulty with which you can get into and out of various keys is determined by their position in the **cycle of fifths**. This is a pictorial way of arranging the keys so they form a sequence. C is at the top. You move clockwise to the dominant, which has one more sharp. Each move in this direction involves another sharp being added to the key signature.

Moving anti-clockwise takes you through the subdominants: each move involves the introduction of a flat.

The sharps and flats meet in the 'middle' so that C sharp and D flat are regarded as being the same. The cycle is only an illusion, however, since if you modulate all the way round there is no feeling of having come back where you started. What is important about it is that it can be used as a sort of table to identify related keys. In the diagram below major keys are in the outer circle with their relative minors inside.

The shape drawn around C shows its closest keys – those to which modulations are the most common.

It is normal for a piece to finish in the same key as it starts. Much tonal music therefore consists of a kind of journey in which you set out, modulate through a series of keys and gradually work your way back home.

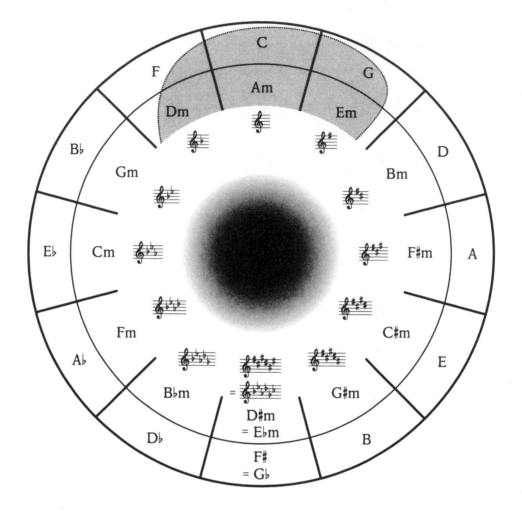

===== **More Ideas** =====

▶ Working with a friend, each write a four-bar melody. Now swap papers and give your friend a destination key to which they have to modulate by composing an answering phrase.

▶ Make a list of related keys using the cycle of fifths as a guide. Now compose a chord progression which modulates through all those keys.

## Chromaticism

A chromatic note is introduced by raising or lowering a degree of the diatonic scale. For many centuries composers have employed this as a device with which to add variety. The last chapter showed how non-essential chromatic notes can add interest to an otherwise basic melodic outline.

In most cases a chromatic note in a chord is resolved like any other dissonance – that is, onto a note in the next chord. In the example below, which is in C major, the subdominant chord is altered by flattening its third. The A flat resolves downwards onto the G.

Chromatic harmony is a very pronounced feature of Romantic music. By the end of this period the style of some composers was so chromatic it became hard to tell what key the music was in. Indeed, Schoenberg pushed tonality to its limits, and developed the twelve-note system (see Chapter 13) based on the chromatic scale.

It is not necessary to have a highly advanced knowledge of harmony to use chromaticism effectively, however. There are a number of ways in which it can be introduced:

## Special cadences

There are a number of 'novelty' cadences. One of these is the **Phrygian cadence**, a type of imperfect cadence which uses a chromatic note when in a major key:

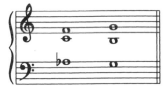

Related to this is the **Neapolitan cadence**. This is an adaptation of the common II–V–I cadence. The supertonic chord is replaced by a chord on the *flattened* supertonic, usually in first inversion:

This chord is so called because the flat supertonic is popularly used as a decoration in Neapolitan folk-song. Another member of this family of chords is the **German sixth**. This is built on the flat submediant as a means of modulating to the dominant:

The chord sounds like a seventh, but the interval from the A flat to the F sharp is written as a sharpened sixth. This is dictated by simple musical grammar: the F sharp resolves upwards to G.

The **diminished seventh** chord consists entirely of minor thirds. It is a very useful chord since it can, when used in place of a normal dominant, resolve in two ways. In the following example a diminished seventh chord is used first to modulate to the relative minor and again to return to the tonic. Note that when the chord first appears the top note is called G sharp because this is the leading note of A minor. On the second appearance the note has to be called A flat because it resolves down onto G.

### Chromatic decoration to the harmony

An otherwise simple harmony can be made more colourful if chromatic passing notes are introduced. In the example below by Schumann the left hand plays a series of thirds, descending in semitones, while the melody also contains chromatic passing notes:

Schumann: *Scenes from Childhood* Op.15 'Frightening'

The basic harmonic structure is actually very simple:

The Chopin Prelude (E minor, opus 28) below has a slightly more complex structure but illustrates a technique which forms the basis of much chromatic harmony (and, incidentally, jazz). This involves resolving one discord onto another. This is easier to understand if you examine a few bars in detail.

Bar 1 – a first inversion of the tonic, E minor.

Bar 2 – the E is held over as a sort of suspension: the ear expects it to resolve onto D sharp, but Chopin notates this as E flat. This forms a diminished seventh chord on the last beat with the right hand C.

Bar 3 – the E flat is held over and the bottom note of the chord falls to F natural. The E flat finally resolves onto D; the A then falls a semitone to G sharp. If the B in the right hand had remained a diminished chord would have been created, but this moves up to C.

Bar 4 – resolves onto an E major chord, but with the D held over as a seventh.

The melody itself is extremely basic, hovering about the dominant like a right hand 'pedal'. Like much chromatic music the underlying chord structure is quite simple:

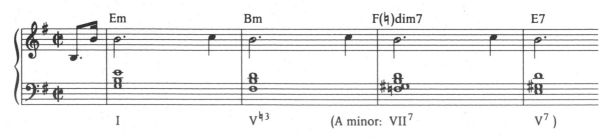

## Rapid modulations

Modulations placed very close together can generate a great sense of drama. The easiest way to construct a series of modulations is in the form of a sequence. This one is from Brahms' *Rhapsody* Opus 79 No. 2:

The basic scheme is as follows:

Brahms adds a range of subtleties to this scheme. The bass line is not quite what you expect. For example the opening, on two first inversion chords, makes you wonder if you are in E flat or G minor – intentionally, of course. This effect is repeated in bars 4–5 where it is hard to tell if you are in G major or B minor. The important thing to learn from this is that chromaticism and modulation are rarely employed as mere decoration but as a way of introducing tension and mystery into the music.

## Exercises using chromatic harmony

Here are some ways of trying out ideas for chromatic harmonies.

Work out a simple broken chord figuration over a bass (the example below is for keyboard but you could do this exercise equally well with two orchestral instruments). Once you are able to play the passage fluently, try altering some of the notes so that each broken chord has a small chromatic 'lead in'.

Try to remember what you have played. Write the figures down and analyse the chords.

Another way to learn about chromatic harmony is to take a chord progression and add chromatic notes. In the example below a passage of four-part harmony is altered by adding chromatic passing notes to the parts.

Why not try composing a short Romantic Fantasy? These pieces were usually quite free in form and often featured displays of instrumental skill.

You may find it helpful first to devise a chord progression.

Then use your progression as the basis for a series of runs and arpeggios. For ways of extending this piece see Chapter 12 on Form.

# CHAPTER ELEVEN

# Counterpoint and texture

In order to compose contrapuntal style studies you will need to have covered some of the introductory work contained in Chapters 4 and 5. You will also need some knowledge of the history of music. This does not need to be highly detailed at this stage but it would help to be aware, for example, that fugue was an invention of the late Baroque and that it would be inappropriate to compose a Bach-type fugue in the style of Palestrina.

The examples below are drawn from techniques and forms which are characteristic of their period. Some historical background is filled in but this should be supported by other reading.

## Modal harmony

Many students begin to study sixteenth-century counterpoint only after they have learnt how to compose in the style of later composers such as Bach. This sometimes means having to 'un-learn' certain ideas which are taken for granted in more modern music. The most important thing to realize is that early composers did not think in terms of chord progressions or in regular phrase lengths.

Sixteenth-century music is never described as being in a key. It is composed in one of several modes (some examples of modes are introduced in Chapter 3). The modal system is a complex one, and learning its intricacies is not made easier by the fact that modern ears find the association with keys and cadences very hard to resist.

The stylistic guidelines for harmony are the same as those outlined in Chapter 10 and are summarized here with a few additions. There should be a consonance (octave, fifth, third or sixth) on each beat, unless a dissonance has been properly prepared. In sixteenth-century polyphony the beat is called the **tactus**. This is an underlying pulse. In modern notation of this type of music the tactus is usually a minim.

▶ The following are not allowed: consective fifths and octaves, exposed fifths and octaves, doubled major thirds.

▶ The perfect fourth is a dissonance; passing six-four chords are not allowed.

▶ Avoid at all costs the interval of the augmented fourth (or diminished fifth, which is the same interval upside down). It must not sound against the bass on a beat:

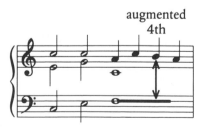

and it must not be 'outlined' by a melody:

Modal harmony was governed by a practice called **musica ficta**. Notes were chromatically altered in order to create a more pleasing (or easy to perform) melody. The term means 'false notes'; in the sixteenth century these alterations were left to the performers and did not appear in the written music. Some typical instances where false notes might be introduced are as follows:

▶ to sharpen a note at the end of a phrase. This often creates a definite cadence effect, and sometimes the feeling of a modulation as well.

▶ to smooth out a phrase on its ascent or descent (you may be familiar with this principle in the use of the melodic minor scale).

After you have thought about some of these rules, try to keep the following points in mind:

▶ Unless you have had a lot of practice at imitating early music styles it can be extremely difficult to tell which mode you are in. You will probably find it helpful to think in keys – the convention of sharpening the leading note usually means that the music approximates to a 'normal' key anyway.

▶ Aim to achieve graceful, independent parts even if this means allowing the harmony to wander. The harmony in most sixteenth-century music tends to revolve around I, IV, V and II.

## The cantus firmus

A great deal of music was composed against a **cantus firmus**. This is a slow melody running through the counterpoint like a sort of backbone. Usually it is a plainchant or a popular melody written out in long notes with more elaborate parts around it. This principle was introduced in Chapter 5 (see species counterpoint). In the example below a plainchant is written out in semibreves. A second part is added above. The words 'Gloria in excelsis' are from the Latin mass. No attempt has been made to plan the chords. It is enough simply to achieve a consonance on each strong beat. Note the B flat in bar 6, introduced to avoid an augmented fourth above the bass.

### Exercise

Try composing some sections of the mass in two parts. Write the cantus first, then add a flowing part above or below.

## Imitation

Imitation is the practice of composing each contrapuntal entry so it imitates the ones before. It is related to the techniques of round and canon, but is treated with more freedom; there is no need to maintain the imitation beyond the first few notes, and it is not necessary for each part to enter on the same note.

When writing imitative counterpoint it is best to follow the advice given in Chapter 5 for composing a canon – write in the entries first, then fill in the other sections. Try writing in two parts, then progress to three. The two-part example below is from the Mass *Douce Memoire* by Lassus. The first half consists of an imitative texture (canonic, in fact) while the second half features a cantus firmus in the upper part with a free part below.

## Exercises

Ask your teacher to provide you with a copy of some sixteenth-century counterpoint in three parts. Copy out a short section from the beginning, leaving out a portion of a part, a whole part or, if you are feeling adventurous, two parts. Have a go at completing the texture. The exercise below is taken from the Benedictus from Palestrina's Mass *Aeterna Christe Munera* and consists of three imitative entries. The alto part is given in full, but only the entries of the other voices.

\* The figure *8* below the clef indicates that this part sounds one octave lower.

Try writing some exercises for instruments rather than voices. One instrumental form which was based on the imitative style of sixteenth-century counterpoint was the **canzona**. Among the best known canzonas are those of the Italian composer Frescobaldi, who lived from 1583 to 1643. The skill of composing a canzona is to produce effortless counterpoint which suggests that the instruments are in an energetic conversation. The example below is by the author. Note how all the entries are in the same rhythm. This particular rhythm is characteristic of the canzona.

## The late Baroque

There can be little doubt that counterpoint in the style of the late Baroque is easier to copy than sixteenth-century counterpoint. The rules are less strict and Baroque music is much more obviously based on chord progressions, keys and modulations.

Start by working in two parts. One helpful place to begin is with the Two-Part Inventions by Bach, because they contain such a wide variety of contrapuntal techniques of which imitation is the most common.

In his Invention No. 4 Bach takes a simple melodic idea which is in two halves:

He then proceeds to construct an opening phrase in which the two halves are repeated and divided between two hands:

Right hand     a   b   a

Left hand          a   b

This is an extremely economical use of the material and is made easy by the harmony, which alternates between I and V (or VII, which can be used in place of V). It would be possible to extend this idea into quite a long passage using this technique.

### Exercise

Compose a set of two-bar phrases based on chords I and V.

Try fitting them together in different ways:

Right hand     A   B   A   C   D   B

Left hand        A   B   D   C   A

Obviously you cannot expect to repeat chords I and V for ever in this way, but so long as you continue to structure the music in two-bar segments it should be possible to write quite a long piece with some variety in it.

## Double counterpoint

Writing two-part phrases in which either of the parts can appear at the top will be easier and more interesting if you master the art of **double counterpoint**. This is counterpoint in which two parts are interchangeable as in the example below, taken from Bach's Invention No. 6. The first four bars are repeated (starting at bar 5) with the two parts swapped over.

With a bit of practice you will find that double counterpoint enables you to get considerable mileage out of a few bars because ideas can be repeated in different ways, sounding like something new when in fact it is an old idea 'repackaged'.

As a beginner you are advised to stick to double counterpoint at the octave. This means that when parts change places the top one goes down an octave (or two) and the bottom one goes up an octave (or two), as in the Bach example. It is possible, however, to compose double counterpoint at any interval. In other words when you swap the parts you transpose one of them as well. The most common example of this is double counterpoint at the twelfth (that is, at an octave plus a fifth).

When composing double counterpoint at the octave you must be familiar with intervals and their inversions, because when you turn the counterpoint upside down you automatically invert the intervals. The following table shows what happens:

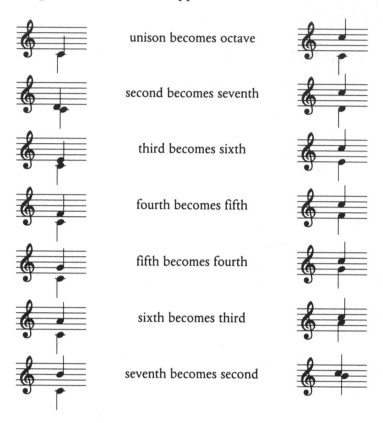

Octaves, thirds and sixths continue to be consonant even when inverted. Dissonant seconds and sevenths should invert without difficulty as long as they are prepared and resolved properly. The problem interval in double counterpoint is the fifth, because it becomes a dissonant fourth when inverted.

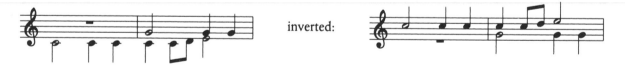

The solution is to try to avoid landing on a bare fifth, and to make sure any fifths you do include are resolved.

You will also need to keep a watch out for parallel fourths which, when inverted, produce consecutive fifths.

Practise double counterpoint by doing some exercises in species counterpoint (see page 42). Write out a melody in semibreves and compose something to go with it which fits both above and below. (Hint: double counterpoint is easier if you write out one of the parts and compose the others around it.)

Write a very simple **chorale prelude**. Choose a chorale melody from a book of chorales and write it out in long note values. Add a decorative part to go with it. This part should be in double counterpoint and in the style of Bach.

## Fugue

Fugue is a form in which composers can display their contrapuntal skill. It developed from the canzona and became particularly popular during the late Baroque, culminating in Bach's two great works dedicated to the form, *The Art of Fugue* and *The Well-Tempered Clavier* (or *Forty-eight Preludes and Fugues*). There are many later examples – Haydn, Mozart and Beethoven all composed fugues, and although there are fewer instances during the Romantic period some twentieth-century composers, including Britten and Shostakovitch, have shown a special fondness for the form.

A typical fugue is based on a fragment of melody, called the **subject**. Subjects need to be memorable so they stand out in the texture, and they often include rhythmic or melodic ideas which can be used as **motifs** later on in the piece to construct other sections.

Next, another part enters. This is called the **answer**; it is the same as (or similar to) the subject, and it enters in the dominant. In other words, if the first note of the subject is C the answer will start on G. (There is an exception, however, and this is explained below – see *tonal answers*.)

As soon as the answer begins the first part provides a melody to go with it, called the **countersubject**. This usually contrasts with the answer in some way. The contrast in the example is mainly rhythmic. Note the modulation in bar 5. Countersubjects often include such a modulation to help the answer establish itself.

Once the answer has finished it is possible to introduce another part with the subject in the tonic again. Entries may continue in this alternating pattern – subject/answer, tonic/dominant – until all the voices have entered (the usual number is three or four). This opening set of entries is called the **exposition**.

After this there is usually a succession of **episodes**, each modulating through a series of keys and sometimes leading to a statement of the subject in a new key. Lastly there is a **final entry** when the subject is heard in the tonic.

There are, obviously, many different types of fugue, and the form really deserves more detailed study than there is space for here.

When you compose your first fugue you should choose a simple subject. To begin with, work in two parts and concentrate on writing a strong exposition. After that you can progress to complete fugues and exercises in three or more parts.

*Tonal answers*

Until you have had some practice, avoid subjects which start on the dominant or which leap to the dominant. In these cases the rules of fugue will oblige you to devise what is know as a **tonal answer**. The rules are as follows:

▶ If the subject starts on the dominant the answer must start, not a fifth higher as you would expect, but on the tonic:

▶ If the subject starts on the tonic and leaps to the dominant the answer must start on the dominant and leap to the tonic:

*A complete fugue*

The illustration example below is a two-part fugue from Bach's *Well-Tempered Clavier*, Book 1, No. 10. Here is a brief analysis.

Exposition

Bar 1    Subject

Bar 3    Answer with countersubject in right hand

**Bar 5**  Episode 1. Based on material from the countersubject. Note the strong progression of chords, with roots moving in fifths towards G: F sharp, B minor, E, A minor, D, G.

**Bar 11**  Subject in G (the relative major)

**Bar 13**  Answer

**Bar 15**  Episode 2. Note the alternating texture: quavers in one part alternating with semiquavers in the other. Episode leads to next entry:

**Bar 20**  Subject in A minor (the subdominant)

**Bar 22**  Answer

**Bar 24**  Episode 3. Like Episode 1, based on material from the countersubject. Leading to next entry:

**Bar 30**  Subject in D minor. This is the key of the flattened leading note and you might expect this to weaken a return to the home key. However, the answer, in A minor (subdominant) brings the progression of keys closer. The modulation back to E minor occurs in the next episode.

**Bar 34**  Episode 4. Based on the texture of Episode 2 (note how Bach creates unity by repeating textures in this way). Modulation leading to final entry is as follows:

|  |  |  |
|---|---|---|
| Bar 34 | E major | (dominant of the last entry in A minor) |
| Bar 35 | A major | (dominant of D) |
| Bar 36 | D major | (dominant of G) |
| Bar 37 | G major | (the relative major) |

**Bar 38**  B major (the dominant of home key E minor)

**Bar 39**  Final entry of subject

Episode 1

Subject (in G major)

(Countersubject)

(Countersubject)                                          Episode 2

Answer

(Countersubject)

Subject (in A minor)

Answer                                                    Episode 3

(Countersubject)

(Countersubject)

Subject (in D minor)

Answer

(Countersubject)

Episode 4

Final entry of Subject

*Hints on fugue writing*

When you write a fugue of your own, sketch the important material first. Then devise a formal plan. You may well need to adapt this as you go along but it helps to have some idea where you are going. Write the exposition first and bring it to a cadence. Then sketch the episodes.

Don't forget that fugues don't have to be written as an exercise for piano. Try writing them for orchestral instruments or make a multi-track recording or play the parts into a *sequencer* (see Chapter 15).

## Continuo

Not all Baroque counterpoint is florid. One very common texture was a melody with a simple bass line, as in this example from one of Bach's *French Suites*:

Apart from the occasional bar of imitation, the bass part treads away solidly below with a combination of broken chords and passing notes. The simplicity of this bass line is a clue to its origins in **continuo**.

Continuo is characteristic of the Baroque and involves two instruments: one to play the bass line (usually a low string instrument) and one to fill in chords (specified in the form of a figured bass, and usually played on a keyboard – organ or harpsichord). This was discussed in the last chapter.

### Exercises using continuo

Compose a melody with continuo along the lines of this example from Bach's cantata *Sleepers Wake*.

You do not need a harpsichord or an organ to play the figured chords – an electronic keyboard could do this (it may even be possible to use the auto-chord function), or they could be strummed by a guitar (you may have to provide chord symbols instead of figured bass). Simple dance movements, like the Bach minuet above, could be composed for flute with a continuo of bass xylophone and guitar.

## Classical textures

The radical difference between Baroque texture and Classical texture is well illustrated by comparing the music of Bach with that of one of his sons, Johann Christian. J C Bach was one of the early Classical composers, and his style is characterized by textures which are bare and bold in comparison with the decorative embellishments of the Baroque.

J C Bach: Sonata, Opus 5 No.1

In the Classical period there was a much clearer distinction between a melody and an accompaniment. The commonest figuration in use as an accompaniment was the 'Alberti bass', named after the early eighteenth-century composer Domenico Alberti who, although he may not actually have invented the figuration, certainly made extensive use of it.

Typically the notes of the chords are broken into regular quavers. It offers a means of playing all (or most of) the notes in a chord and, at the same time, keeping the rhythm on the move.

There are many variations on this figure to be found in Classical music. Some are similar to Baroque figurations while others exploit the percussive sound of the recently invented forte-piano with its modern hammer action.

A simpler and very dramatic accompaniment was the repeated note. Quite often the strong beats would be emphasized by playing the note down an octave.

Repeated-note accompaniments like these were often used as a **pedal**. This device, based on the drone, creates a great sense of drama and urgency because of the dissonances between the changing chords and the bass.

In addition to emphasizing the difference between melody and accompaniment, the Classical period was characterized by contrast of texture. Sometimes these contrasts were quite extreme; a passage in octaves might be followed by some counterpoint, then by a melody with Alberti bass.

Compose a short melody for piano using techniques discussed in the previous chapter. Write out the melody for the right hand and add an Alberti-type bass in the left. Check that the notes all lie comfortably under the hand.

Make a list of three or more textures – for example, Alberti bass, octaves, chords, unaccompanied melody. Now write a short piece which passes through all these types. Study some piano sonatas by Haydn, Mozart and Beethoven. See how many different types of texture you can see.

## *The string quartet*

One four-part texture worth studying is the string quartet (two violins, viola and cello). This established itself in the Classical period as a favoured medium through which composers could express their more serious thoughts. For this reason, and because it is based on a four-part harmonic texture, it tends to come up quite frequently in exams, usually taking the form of a completion. (You will be given a short extract with one or more parts missing, which have to be filled in in accordance with the style.)

One way for the beginner to approach string writing is through the early quartets of Haydn, the textures of which are less complicated than they appear. Many of the faster movements are in fairly simple two-part counterpoint, the violins playing one part in octaves and the viola and cello playing the other part in octaves.

Minuet II from Haydn: String Quartet Op. 1 No.3

Some quartet writing consists of a melody and accompaniment. In the example below the first violin plays the melody, violin II and viola share an Alberti figure and the cello plays the bass. Note that the viola part is written using the **alto clef**.

Writing four truly independent parts takes a little practice. The ideal quartet texture consists of a conversation between four individuals, rather than a counterpoint of equal parts or a melody with support. Here is part of a minuet movement by Beethoven (from his quartet Opus 18 No. 5).

The four-part harmony is brought to life by being played in three different ways: violin I plays the melody, the inner two parts (violin II and viola) have long, legato notes and the bass (cello) is a repeated pedal.

## Exercises

Listen to some quartets with the score in front of you. You will probably be surprised how many rests there are in each part and how much 'breathing space' there is in the music.

Ask your teacher to find some easier examples and try playing them on whatever instruments are available.

Try some completions. Take some quartet examples and copy them out with some parts missing. Complete the missing parts. Then try copying out the first four bars of all four parts and see if you can add some further bars of your own.

## Romantic textures

Studying Romantic style is not merely a question of writing Classical music that is 'difficult to play'. For one thing, as you will have seen in the previous chapter, the harmonies are different; there are more chromatic notes and dissonances. Also, and just as important, there was a change in the outlook of composers. The Romantics were much more concerned about expressing moods and feelings. The nocturne below, by the Irish composer John Field, is not especially difficult to play. But the chords are spread, using the sonority of the piano keyboard, and this makes the solo melody appear rather isolated and plaintive. It adds up to a very personal statement.

[116]

Unless you are a very good instrumental player and are familiar with the more difficult areas of the Romantic repertoire, it might be better to approach Romantic style study via short character pieces like this.

Figurations are quite easy to find if you study composers like Schumann and Chopin. Chopin's *Berceuse* (lullaby) is a shining example of how many different patterns can be constructed over a simple repeating ostinato:

Texture was important to the Romantics because they used music to paint pictures and create moods.

Listen to the overture from Weber's opera *Der Freischütz*. This is an early Romantic opera about the supernatural, and the music is full of menace, achieved by scoring for instruments in their lowest and darkest registers.

It is possible to suggest pictures without the resources of the full orchestra. In the two following examples Schumann depicts *The Wild Horseman* and *Hide and Seek* (from his *Album for the Young*).

## Exercises

Compose a nocturne for piano in the style of John Field. Aim at a ternary form with the A section being a graceful melody with arpeggio accompaniment in the left hand. Compose a middle section which contrasts with this: it could be in the relative minor and agitated in mood, with jerky rhythms or swirling chromatic scales.

Think of a fanciful title like 'Raindrops', 'Butterflies' or 'Goodbye' and compose a short Schumannesque piece.

## Lieder

**Lieder** is the name given to German art songs in the nineteenth century. They are normally for voice and piano and some of the most famous are by Schubert, who pioneered the art of accompaniments which painted images around the words. In one of his early songs, *Gretchen at the Spinning Wheel*, the piano imitates the whirring wheel.

Schubert: *Gretchen am Spinnrade*, Op. 2

Translation: My peace is gone, my heart is heavy.

## Exercise

Listen to some Schubert songs and then try setting a short poem to music. Choose a poem with a steady metre. Write it out on a sheet of exercise paper. Leave a gap between the lines and, when you think you have some idea of the rhythm, write the note values out above the lines of verse. The example below is from *Song* by the early nineteenth-century poet George Darley.

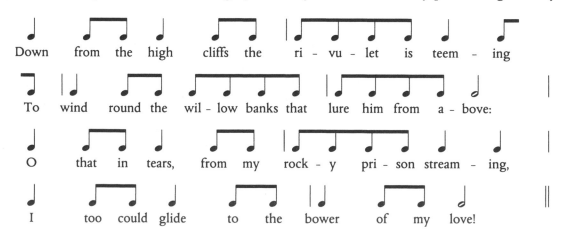

Note that the bars sometimes overlap the lines of verse (for instance at the start of line 2).

[118]

Now try adding notes to your rhythms. Sing them through to yourself (or in your head) to see if the notes you have chosen fit the mood of the words. For a sad subject you could choose a minor key.

If you get really stuck sing the words through to a repeated note. Then, alter the notes one by one until you arrive at a shape you like (this basic technique for composing melody is described in Chapter 2). You may find it helpful to study settings of words to see how they fit with the music. Things to watch for are:

➤ On which word of the line is the accent?
➤ How many notes per syllable?
➤ Where does the melody rise and fall?

Now write out your melody with words on a sheet of manuscript paper, leaving space for the piano part. Then mark in the chords you think will fit.

Lastly, complete the piano part. Here the figurations consist of descending arpeggios to suggest the falling water and tears.

Down from the high cliffs the ri - vu - let is teem - ing, To wind round the wil - low banks that lure him from a - bove: O that in tears, from my rock - y pri - son stream - ing, I too could glide to the bower of my love!

# CHAPTER TWELVE

# Form

The examples of form covered in Chapter 7 were all structures within which a piece of music could be written with a minimum of compositional skill. The examples in this chapter are a little more demanding although they are not uniformly difficult. Some forms, like sets of variations and the chaconne, require melodic invention. Others, like binary and sonata form, require a fair degree of confidence with harmony – especially the ability to modulate.

It is very important to study and analyse lots of music so you can understand how it is constructed. Don't be afraid to rewrite sections of other composers' music; you could write out the first half of a piece and invent a new second half. Or you could write out a blank score of a piece with just the chord progressions and cadences sketched in and then compose new ideas to fit the composer's original scheme. Excercises of this type are called stylistic completions and are sometimes set as tests. This chapter is not about how to do completions but how to compose whole pieces. If you can do this you ought to find the tests easy. The examples are introduced in order of composing difficulty rather than historical order.

## Theme and variations

Sets of variations have always been popular with composers, perhaps because it is a chance to borrow and adapt music from another composer without being accused of plagiarism. The theme is usually played at the beginning in a straightforward fashion and then repeated a number of times, each repetition bearing some alteration or elaboration.

The examples below are taken from a set of variations by Mozart. The tune has since become very well known in English as *Twinkle, twinkle little star*.

Mozart: Variations in C, K. 265

Variation 1 consists of decorating the melody by weaving auxiliaries and passing notes around it (these *non-essential* notes are explained in Chapter 5).

Variation 2 retains the melody in the right hand, decorated with a sequence of suspensions, and greatly elaborates the left hand accompaniment.

Variation 3 takes the basic chords and builds arpeggios and passing notes on them in a triplet rhythm.

Variation 5 introduces rhythmic variety. The melody notes themselves are largely unaltered.

## Exercise

Following Mozart's example try a set of variations of your own. Write a melody and add an accompaniment. Then try some of the following ideas:

► Decorate the melody with runs and ornaments

► Alter the rhythm of the melody

► Build broken chords and arpeggios around the harmony

► Compose different accompaniment figurations

► Write the melody in the left hand and put something above

► Add a countermelody

Why not try something really adventurous? Write a set of variations which exploits different techniques and styles of music: canons, popular music styles, Romantic harmonies. The American composer Charles Ives wrote a set of variations on *America* (the same tune as the English national anthem) some of which were based on popular dances.

## The ground bass, chaconne and passacaglia

Compositions built on a repeated bass line were popular throughout the Baroque and have their origins in Renaissance dance music.

One type of piece, common in the sixteenth and seventeenth centuries, was a set of variations built on a repeating fragment of a scale or mode. The fragment was often six notes long, for example C D E F G A. The piece might be called *Fantasia on Ut Re Mi Fa Sol La* – these note names representing an early form of tonic solfa. A simple example, by the author, appears below, with the six notes repeating in the left hand and decorations in the right.

These fantasias contributed to the development of the **chaconne**, which is structured the same way – a repeated bass line with a series of new ideas and variations above it. Many chaconnes involve bass lines of four or eight bars – rarely longer – and one feature of the repeating harmony is that it allows countless opportunites for contrapuntal imitation, including canon, as in this example from Corelli's Trio Sonata Opus IV No. 12.

Some music dictionaries define **passacaglia** as being similar to a chaconne with the exception that the repeated phrase does not have to appear in the bass all the time. However, composers treated both these terms with great freedom. Whatever you decide to call your composition, the option of moving your repeated phrase to an inner part or featuring it as a melody provides an opportunity for more variations.

## Exercise

Compose a chaconne or passacaglia in which a repeated phrase appears in different parts.

Decide on a structure – perhaps the phrase could start off in the bass, work its way up through the inner parts to the treble and then back down again. You may find it helpful to compose each repetition on a separate page so you can shuffle them around and experiment with different versions.

A bass line descending by step could be used as a theme. Sketch this in at different registers leaving blanks for the other part (or parts).

During the course of the 25 bars outlined in the example below the theme appears in the bass (repeated), the middle part (repeated) the top part and, finally, in the bass.

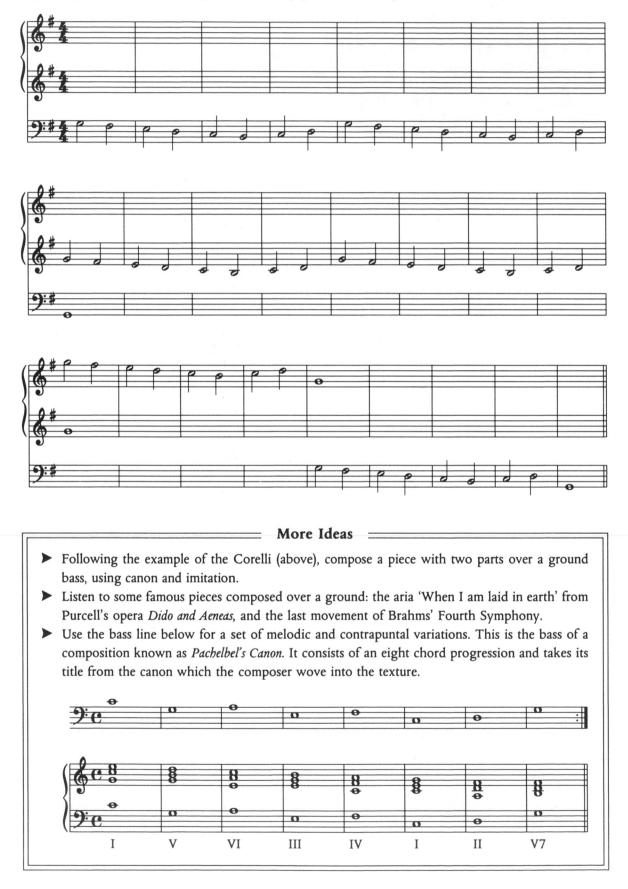

## More Ideas

► Following the example of the Corelli (above), compose a piece with two parts over a ground bass, using canon and imitation.

► Listen to some famous pieces composed over a ground: the aria 'When I am laid in earth' from Purcell's opera *Dido and Aeneas*, and the last movement of Brahms' Fourth Symphony.

► Use the bass line below for a set of melodic and contrapuntal variations. This is the bass of a composition known as *Pachelbel's Canon*. It consists of an eight chord progression and takes its title from the canon which the composer wove into the texture.

## Binary form

**Binary form** was commonly used in the Baroque and was the standard form for most dance movements. It is the forerunner of **sonata form**.

As the name suggests, it is in two halves. The end of the first half is marked by a modulation to the dominant (if the piece is in the minor the modulation will be to the relative major). At this point it is usual to repeat the first half.

The function of the second half is to balance the first; it is usually the same length and brings the music to a close in the tonic. The music often passes through a few related keys on the way. Like the first, this half is also repeated.

The courante below, by Corelli, is typical. Here it is written out for piano, although the original was for two violins with a continuo of cello and harpsichord.

### Exercise in binary form

Perhaps the simplest approach to composing a piece in binary form is to work melodically, planning the modulations as you go and using techniques discussed in Chapters 9 and 10. As in any exercise in form, it is important to know where you are going, so you might find it helpful to sketch out the melody first.

Try playing the piece with and without repeats. Is there any difference? In most binary forms the piece usually sounds stronger when the two halves are repeated.

---

## More Ideas

Compose a suite of dances for keyboard. It would be worth studying two collections by Bach, the *French Suites* and the *English Suites*. Each dance had its own character, but almost all are in binary form.

---

## Sonata form

**Sonata form** became the standard form in the Classical period and is the basis of the symphony, concerto and chamber music as well as the solo sonata. It is related to binary form but is different because of the way modulation is treated.

In binary form the first half concludes with a cadence in the dominant, but it does not really feel as if this key is there to stay: the listener is aware of the need for more music, eventually leading back to the tonic.

In sonata form there is also a move to the dominant, but the modulation is much more decisive and actually establishes the dominant as a new-sounding key. This is achieved by modulating to the **dominant of the dominant** with the result that the original tonic loses its 'pull'.

Sonata form tends to fall into three sections:

### The exposition
This consists of an opening theme (or themes) in the tonic, followed by a passage modulating to the dominant and known as the **transition**. Once the new key is established there is a second theme (or themes). The exposition ends with a cadence in the new key.

### The development
There is no fixed length for a development, nor a fixed number of sections. It usually involves melodies and other ideas drawn from the exposition, and leads to the third and final section via a sequence of modulations to the tonic.

### The recapitulation
This is a repetition of the exposition, but with an important difference: the transition has to be re-written slightly so that the second theme or themes stay in the tonic (otherwise the movement would end in the dominant and fail to get 'home').

Sometimes there is an extra section at the very end called the **coda**. The purpose of the coda is to finish the movement off conclusively and neatly.

## Composing an exposition

The worked example below (by the author) takes the Classical melody given as an example in Chapter 9, page 84, as a starting point. You may find it helpful to turn back to read how it was initially constructed.

The first theme is as follows, here harmonized in the form of a piano sonata:

The difficult part to compose is the transition, and it is important to be clear where this is going. In the case of this example in C major we need to compose a passage of music ending in the dominant of the dominant – that is, a perfect cadence in D.

Many transitions are constructed around sequences because they tend to be easier to 'steer'. This example includes a sequence starting in bar 13 onto which a transition can be built. It involves a bass line heading towards D.

The transition cadence is added by introducing a chord popular with classical composers, the chord of the augmented sixth. In this example the chord is used in the form of a chromatic passing note in the bass (E flat) over which the sixth chord is built. This resolves into the chord of D, which is then stressed by repetition. The example below starts at bar 17.

You do not need to employ chromatic harmony, however, but could choose a more conventional V – I cadence. The example below is an alternative transition. Here, the passage modulates first to G (using the F sharp in the bass) and then to D (using the C sharp in the melody).

The second theme (in the dominant, G) should now follow naturally. It is a test of a successful transition that this theme sounds comfortable in its new key, and this is one reason why the dominant of the dominant has to be stressed.

The second theme is often gentler than the opening one, doubtless because of the need for peace after the drama of the transition. But, as in any artistic process, there are no hard and fast rules. Mozart and Haydn often composed not one second subject but a succession of melodies, and Beethoven was fond of second subjects in keys a third away from the tonic. The example below, however, is a straightforward melody in four-bar phrases in the dominant:

At this point you need to play all the sections composed so far to see how they fit together. In particular you should listen carefully to the end of the exposition. Does it finish abruptly? If so, can this be solved simply by repeating the second theme? Or is it necessary to add a codetta (a small coda appearing at the end of the section)? Such questions can only be answered by testing, trial and error.

The full exposition is given opposite. Note the repetition of most of the second theme at bar 30, and also the codetta at bar 33 with its longer note values – these have the effect of slowing down the pace like a sort of rhythmic brake.

## Composing a development

Developments are usually based on melodies taken from the exposition, although it is not uncommon for completely new material to be introduced. The beginning of the development provides an opportunity to exploit the unexpected; composers are fond of plunging the music into remote keys without warning.

If you want to try a surprise of that sort, don't forget that everything in a sonata plays a part in the overall scheme of things. In experimenting with remote keys you should have some idea what relationship they have to the home key (however distant), since one of the most important functions of the development is to prepare the way for the recapitulation in the tonic.

[128]

Allegro

The example below starts with the opening theme (in G) and immediately transposes it into a new key (B flat). This is followed by statements of the second theme, firstly in E flat and then in C minor. There is then a modulation to G, the dominant of the home key. This is stressed as a pedal, the effect of which is to build up the listener's expectations and thus to pave the way for the recapitulation, of which the first part is shown.

The choice of keys in the development needs explaining. The key of the second theme – E flat – is important because its relative minor is C minor. The route back to the home key is thus via its *minor* form. This represents one of many, many possible routes back to the home key. The route you choose will depend upon your knowledge of related keys and a study of the cycle of fifths. Unless you feel confident rambling through a series of distantly related keys, keep your route simple.

## Composing a recapitulation

This starts exactly like the exposition, but the transition needs to be altered. This needs to modulate to and stress the dominant (and not continue on to the dominant of the dominant as it did before). Usually this means adapting the original harmonies slightly so the second theme can follow in the home key.

The second theme is now in the home key (bar 85). You might ask why it is necessary to have a transition if both themes are in the same key. There are two reasons. One is balance: the recapitulation needs to match the exposition. The other reason is that the transition here serves further to reinforce the home key.

As with the exposition, you will need to play the whole movement through a few times to check that it ends conclusively. It would be pity if, after all this work, it merely fizzled out. A coda may help, perhaps some virtuoso scales and a grand final cadence.

## Exercises in sonata form

Before you tackle a full-sized sonata movement of your own you should analyse some sonata movements by Classical composers. The first movement of Mozart's string serenade *Eine Kleine Nachtmusik* is popular as an introduction to the form.

Pay particular attention to the character of the main themes, the ways in which the texture is varied and, most of all, the harmonies and construction of the transition, since this is arguably the most difficult section to compose. Write out the harmonies and identify the way in which the new key is established.

When you compose a pastiche example try to keep in mind the style of the composer you are copying. Concentrate on writing vivid and interesting thematic material.

## Romantic forms

Although Classical forms like the sonata persisted into the Romantic period, composers tended to devise names for their pieces to suggest an element of compositional freedom: impromptu, fantasy, novelette, intermezzo. Sometimes compositions depicted particular moods or scenes, like the nocturne (see Chapter 11), and some composers, particularly Chopin and Brahms, developed a fondness for dances. Most of these compositions were on a small scale and might be grouped together under the general heading of **character pieces**. Some ideas for composing examples of these are introduced at the end of Chapters 10 and 11.

The form of the character piece was not particularly new – in fact most examples tend to be in ternary form. The difficulties in composing them are caused not so much by the forms as by the complexities of Romantic harmony and the technical demands of performance.

If you intend to try composing some Romantic miniatures you should listen to and study some examples. Among the shortest and most accessible are the *Moments Musicaux* by Schubert and the many short pieces by Schumann, especially *Scenes from Childhood*. Mendelssohn's *Songs Without Words*, written for the piano, are also worth looking at.

The form of such pieces tends to be quite simple – ternary or binary. Sometimes pieces were held together more by mood than the principles of repetition, for example Chopin's Nocturne opus 15 in G minor.

## Exercises

Compose a set of short, simple pieces for a young child learning the piano. You may find it helpful to get some ideas from Schumann's children's pieces.

Compose some dances for piano. Listen to some waltzes by Chopin and Brahms and see if you can imitate some of the Romantic harmonies.

You could also try writing a **mazurka**. This Polish dance was a great favourite of Chopin (he wrote over 50). Many are quite simple in texture and form, but all tend to feature the mazurka's characteristic rhythm:

Chopin: Mazurka Op. 7 No. 1

Chopin: Mazurka Op. 41 No. 2

*Programme music*

Programme music – music that tells a story – had been popular with composers for centuries before the Romantic period. Couperin composed pieces for clavichord depicting jugglers, monkeys and bears, and there are numerous instances in the religious music of Bach and Handel where pictures are being painted in sound.

However, the Romantics were influenced by the moods, form and structure of stories far more than their predecessors. The **ballad** was based on the drama and emotions of epic poetry, and the examples by Brahms and, particularly, Chopin, are large-scale pieces comparable with a sonata.

These forms led, later in the nineteenth century, to the **tone poem** (this is discussed in Chapter 15 as well). Here the composition is inspired by a story or picture and the form is based upon the feelings and images evoked.

Romantic composers tended to find passionate, larger-than-life stories and characters attractive. Listen to Berlioz's two great symphonic poems, *Symphonie Fantastique* (about the dreams of a young artist) and *Harold in Italy* (based on Byron's poem *Childe Harold*).

Choose a story with a 'big' theme: perhaps a poem like Tennyson's *Morte d'Arthur*, or a story from the bible, an ancient legend or a Shakespearian drama. See if you can reduce the story to six or so key scenes or episodes. Compose a piece based on these six sections.

You may find it helpful to adopt a device used by Berlioz in his *Symphonie Fantastique*. A short theme, depicting the beloved of the main character with whom he is obsessed, keeps returning as if to haunt him. Its return also has the effect of creating repetition and unity although, unlike the repetition of melody in Baroque and Classical music, this is a story-telling device.

# Part IV

# The Twentieth Century

During the twentieth century composers freed themselves not only of the need to write music in keys, but also from regular metre and rhythm. The result is that much of the music sounds chromatic and complicated, and it is probably hard to imagine how a relative beginner might approach composing it.

The chapters in this section are a step-by-step guide. Chapter 13 deals with different systems you can employ for finding the notes themselves, whether they are consonant, dissonant, tonal, chromatic, or atonal. Chapter 14 shows how to combine these notes with rhythms to build small phrases and structures. Chapter 15 shows ways of constructing complete pieces and includes an introduction to some styles and genres, like neo-classicism and electro-acoustic composition.

CHAPTER THIRTEEN

# Tonality and atonality

## The whole-tone scale

One of the earliest ways in which composers broke away from traditional tonality was the exploration of systems not based on the major and minor scale, for example the whole-tone scale.

The lack of semitones in this scale give it a very characteristic sound; there is obviously no dominant or subdominant and the chords which can be built from it are all augmented (i.e. major chords in which the fifth is sharpened).

Music based purely on this scale has a dreamy quality with little sense of direction even when there is a regular metre.

Clearly there is a limit to the time you could expect to wander about like this since the vagueness could become quite irritating. One composer who made use of the scale successfully was Debussy; his prelude for piano, *Voiles*, is based entirely on the whole-tone scale, and in other pieces it is used in combination with other scales which introduce variety to the sound and allow a mix of major and minor chords on the degrees of the scale.

Debussy also employed **enharmonic** chord changes. This means taking the top note of a chord and finding different chords to go underneath, regardless of what 'key' they are from.

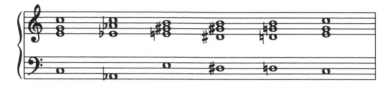

## Modes

A number of composers, particularly Bartók and Stravinsky, have written very chromatic tonal music by combining different modes.

Some modes based on the diatonic scale of C were introduced in Chapter 3. The ones in the examples below are also based on the diatonic scale. You will see that each is in a different key, but that each begins on C.

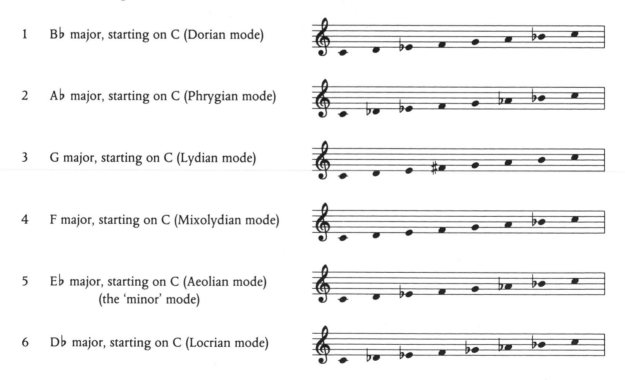

1    B♭ major, starting on C (Dorian mode)

2    A♭ major, starting on C (Phrygian mode)

3    G major, starting on C (Lydian mode)

4    F major, starting on C (Mixolydian mode)

5    E♭ major, starting on C (Aeolian mode)
     (the 'minor' mode)

6    D♭ major, starting on C (Locrian mode)

The following example is a dance – a melody over an ostinato – and it is based on the modes above. For the first four bars the melody is in the last of the six modes shown above; then it switches to a Lydian-type mode (no. 3 above). The bass line, however, is in yet another mode – no. 4 above – and it is this simultaneous sounding of two different modes that makes this music sound chromatic.

## Exercise

Try writing a simple piece of film music using these modes. Choose either a dance for an animal cartoon (along the lines of Walt Disney's *Fantasia*) or something for a suspense story (a walk through a foggy graveyard, perhaps).

You could try inventing your own scales, or adapting existing ones.

Scales do not have to consist of seven different notes: more are possible. The scales below employ eight and are thus called **octatonic scales**. Each is based on a particular intervallic combination of alternating tones and semitones.

=== More Ideas ===

> ► The two scales above, along with the whole tone scale, form part of a set identified by the French composer Messiaen as **modes of limited transposition**. Check, and discover that compared with the major scale, of which there are twelve possible versions, these modes exist in fewer versions. There are, for example, only two versions of the whole tone scale. Investigate this by writing one out and then trying different transpositions.
> ► Invent an octatonic scale and compose a canon whose melody is based on the scale.
> ► If you have studied fugue (see Chapter 11) try writing a fugal exposition using a mode of your choice.
> ► Listen to and study the dances in Stravinsky's ballet *Agon*, and also the piano pieces in Bartók's *Mikrokosmos* (there are six volumes graded by ability). Identify the modes used by both composers.

Composing with chromatic scales sometimes gives rise to music whose general sound might be described as 'Classical music with wrong notes'. There is a temptation to write major/minor harmonies and to construct phrases and accompaniments according to the Classical idiom. One way Bartók avoided this was to adopt irregular metres and rhythms derived from Hungarian dance, thus avoiding any hint of Classical rhythmic structures (e.g. regular metre, four-bar phrases, rhythmic repetition and sequences).

Another way to avoid a Classical feel is to develop a system for using the harmonies which avoids identifying a tonic. Avoid anything which suggests a V–I cadence, perhaps by using several transpositions of the mode at once, or by using augmented chords, which do not normally have a strong sense of harmonic direction.

## Atonality

Atonal music employs chromatic scales in such a way that the music is not in a key at all. The commonest and best-known technique for composing atonal music is 12-note composition.

The basis of 12-note composition is the **note-row**. This consists of all twelve notes of the chromatic scale arranged in a sequence of the composer's choosing.

The row is then used as a 'list' of notes from which the piece is composed. The notes are taken in strict order without repetition, the idea being that if any note is repeated before its turn it will be more prominent than the others and risk the possibility of being heard as a tonic.

In the piece below the notes are numbered according to their order in the row. The example is intended to show how the row can be used to provide both melody and chords, although ways of constructing 12-note music are covered more fully in Chapter 15.

Obviously the type and combination of intervals within the row plays an important part in the eventual sound of the music. For example, a row consisting mainly of consonant intervals will tend to produce consonant music; so one way of controlling whether the overall sound of a composition is predominatly consonant or dissonant is to limit the types of interval you use.

### Constructing a note row

Decide on two intervals. In this example we will choose minor seconds and minor thirds – that is, one dissonant and one consonant interval. The twelve notes are arranged here in four groups of three. Each group of three contains our two chosen intervals.

Obviously there will be a need to vary the row, otherwise the piece will consist of endless repetitions of the same order of notes. Taking the row above the following variations are possible:

1 reversing the row (known as the retrograde)

2 inverting it (writing it upside down – thus if the first interval is a rising minor third the inversion will start with a falling minor third)

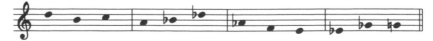

3  writing out the inversion backwards (known as retrograde inversion)

These variations are customarily identified by letters:

O   the row in its original form
R   retrograde
I   inversion
RI  retrograde inversion

Each of these forms can be transposed to a different note of the chromatic scale giving a total of 48 different variations of the row. These are usually identified by a number, with the original row being identified as $O^0$. The untransposed versions of the other forms of the row (inversion, retrograde, etc.) would thus be numbered $I^0$, $R^0$ and so on.

… and so on.

Some composers like to write out all 48 variations in the form of a table but, just as a painter does not always use all the colours in the paint box, so there is no need to use all 48 versions of the row. You are free to pick and choose. Indeed some composers treat serial composition with great freedom. Stravinsky came to serialism late in life, and did not allow any of its limitations to hinder his style. He often left out notes in the row, added new ones and repeated others according to how he wished the music to sound.

## Exercise: composing with a note row

Write a short piece which combines several versions of the row at the same time.

The example below is a two-part canon with accompanying chords and is based on the row in example 17 above. The top line of the canon uses the row in original form. The bottom line of the canon uses a transposition ($O^1$). The chords are made up of notes from the inversion.

► Practise constructing rows. You may find it helpful to start with smaller rows of, perhaps, six notes. Study Stravinsky's *In Memorian Dylan Thomas*, which uses a small row.

► Practise composing chord progressions using a 12-note row. See if you can control the amount of consonance/dissonance by the intervals you choose.

► Study Webern's *Variations* for piano. See if you can identify the note row and the versions of it which the composer uses in the first page.

## Other atonal systems

Serialism, because it treats all the notes of the chromatic scale equally, clearly has built-in safeguards against the music being in a key. It could be argued that any system which allows the possibility of repeated notes, octaves or tonal-sounding melodies and chords cannot be described as a truly atonal one. Composers today are far less strict than they were when serialism was first developed and when some were anxious to avoid any trace of tonality. Today we could be described as being in the age of **pantonality**, where it is possible in a composition to hint at one key or many, to be solidly in a key or not to be in a key at all.

The systems described below are extremely flexible. Some are related to serialism and some have developed from other areas of music, for example bell-ringing.

### Chance

You can devise rows according to chance rather than the methodical approach described above. It is possible to use a pair of dice, dominoes or playing cards in such a way that the spots or numbers stand for the twelve notes of the chromatic scale.

Write out a chromatic scale starting on C and number the notes: C is 1, C sharp is 2, D is 3 and so on.

For a 12-note row you will need a pair of dice. You will need to throw a single dice for notes numbered 1–6 and two dice for notes numbered 7–12. If you throw six singles and six doubles there is a chance you will select all twelve notes although this is unlikely. Decide whether to begin with a single or double throw. The first throw gives the number of the first note. If this is 9, then the first note of the row will be G sharp. Continue this procedure for the other notes.

Obviously there is a chance that some notes will be repeated. You have to decide whether to allow for this – you could, for example, choose to ignore repetitions and keep throwing the dice until you obtained twelve different results. This principle applies to the next examples too.

Still using the note-numberings above lay a set of dominoes face down on the table. Decide how many notes you want in the row, then pick up that number of domino pieces. Adding up the number of spots on each domino will give you the note numbers. If you use all the domino pieces you are likely to get duplications. For example this six note row – 4, 8, 3, 10, 4, 2 – will result in two E flats. You have to decide if this matters or whether you wish to limit the number of domino pieces in order to reduce the chances of this happening.

Remove the kings from a set of playing cards. There are now four twelve-card suits (Ace stands for 1, Jack for 11, Queen for 12). For a set of four 12-note rows deal out four hands of cards. By checking off the numbers in each hand you can write out your four rows. There is no guarantee that each hand will contain a full twelve-note row. If you wish to have more control over the chance process you can devise ways of 'cheating' as you deal.

## Permutation

Permutation means changing the order of a set of things and there are many techniques for achieving this. Usually it is the pitches that are changed, but note values, rhythms and even dynamics can be permutated as well.

### *Rotation*

This is a term associated with 12-note composition and refers to ways in which notes or groups of notes in a row can be re-ordered.

The simplest method is to take a note from the beginning of a row and move it to the back. Some composers divide the row into two and work each half seperately.

A more complicated approach involves dividing up a row into smaller segments and re-ordering each segment individually. If we start with this row:

The notes in each group can be ordered in six possible ways. The following example shows this for the first segment:

It is thus possible to draw up a table with the row at the top and its various rotations underneath.

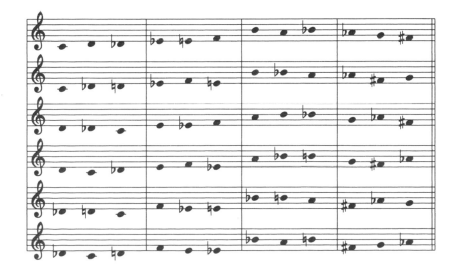

Such a table – some composers refer to it as a **note matrix** – could be used to decide on the versions of a row which you wished to use in a composition, or it could be used to find notes for ostinati, or fragments with which to compose a melody.

## Exercise

Compose a minimalist piece (see Chapter 5) using atonal ostinati. Use the rotation systems described above to create variation in your ostinati.

*Bell ringing*

The principles of changing the order of notes as described above are related to those of bell ringing, or **change ringing** as it is sometimes called. Church bells are usually arranged in scales, and ringing them involves working though the scale in different orders according to a mathematical formula. The ringers refer to this as a 'peal'. There are many different types of peal; each has its own name and – although ringers will usually work for three hours at the most – a complete peal, if left to run, can take days to complete. The foundations of bell-ringing technique were laid down by Fabian Stedman who, in 1668, published the famous bell ringer's handbook *Tintinalogia*.

The examples below show the general principles. Most bell ringers would employ patterns more complicated than this.

The simplest technique is called *hunting*. Here, the first bell changes places one move at a time until it is rung at the end.

What you would hear might sound like this:

[142]

More complicated are *doubles*. In the example below the set of bells is divided into two. Bells 1–3 'hunt' as in the example above. Of the bells in the second half, 4 and 5 change places (this is called 'dodging') and 6 remains static as a reference point for the ringers.

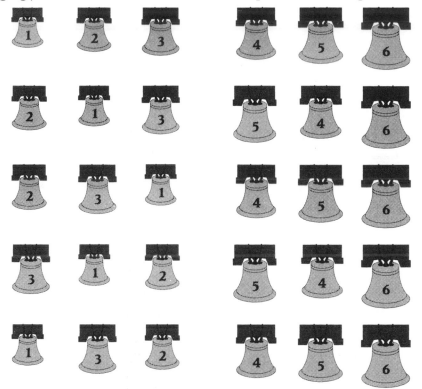

Such a scheme might be applied to a six-note row to change the order of the notes.

[143]

---

### Exercise

Devise a five-note peal for a group of tuned percussion instruments.

## Proportions and numerical series

Numbers can be employed to devise sequences of notes. For example, if 1 equals a semitone then the series 1 5 3 8 1 2 would result in the following set of intervals:

It would also be possible to write out a chromatic scale or a note-row and to select (or delete) notes according to a rule.

Select every third note:

Delete every other note:

Proportions and numerical series have an additional and very obvious application when working with rhythm. This is covered in the next chapter, along with exercises.

## Magic squares

Magic squares sometimes appear in novelty and puzzle books although they were highly regarded by mathematicians in the ancient world. Some writers have suggested that both the pyramids of Egypt and Stonehenge were built according to proportions derived from magic squares.

A typical magic square is a set of numbers arranged in a box like a crossword. Usually the lines, columns and diagonals all add up to the same number, as in the example below, the Square of Saturn. Here the sum of the numbers in all directions is 15:

| 4 | 9 | 2 |
|---|---|---|
| 3 | 5 | 7 |
| 8 | 1 | 6 |

It is possible simply to allocate a note to each box in the square by numbering the notes of a chromatic scale starting on C. With C as 0 the box translates as follows:

| E | A | D |
|---|---|---|
| E♭ | F | G |
| A♭ | D♭ | G♭ |

Three-note groups can be formed by reading in any direction. Alternatively the square can be read spiral fashion; start at one corner and work towards the middle. This is easier if you use a bigger square, such as the Square of Mars.

| 11 | 24 | 7 | 20 | 3 |
|----|----|---|----|---|
| 4 | 12 | 25 | 8 | 16 |
| 17 | 5 | 13 | 21 | 9 |
| 10 | 18 | 1 | 14 | 22 |
| 23 | 6 | 19 | 2 | 15 |

| B♭ | B | F♯ | G | D |
|----|---|----|---|---|
| E♭ | B | C | G♯ | D♯ |
| E | E | C | G♯ | G♯ |
| A | F | C | C♯ | A |
| B♭ | F | F♯ | C♯ | D |

Squares could be used to devise chords. The notes of the chords are obtained by reading down or across the table. The set below is based on the Square of Saturn. Chords are numbered, crossword style, according to the box in which the chord originates.

1 down          2 across          3 down

## Exercises

Look up some magic squares in maths books, or in books such as *The View Over Atlantis*. Devise some ways of using magic squares to generate note rows, rhythms, forms.

Devise a piece in which three players improvise on notes provided by a magic square. Your score could involve an element of graphic notation.

## Chord constructions

Not everyone composes music starting with the individual notes. Some prefer to think in chords and intervals.

Tonal harmony is built on the interval of the third, and many composers have tried building chords in other ways. The Russian composer Scriabin used fourths, inventing a 'mystic chord' which consisted of perfect fourths as well as diminished and augmented fourths.

Here are some examples of chords based on Scriabin's mystic chord.

Chords employing fourths are quite common in twentieth-century music, probably because the fourth is such a versatile interval. It can be made to suggest a key just as easily as it can support atonal textures. It is also quite warm and sonorous compared with chords made up of more dissonant intervals, which can tend to sound cold and thin.

Some composers have used harmonies drawn from the major and minor scales with considerable freedom. The result, which has been described as **pandiatonic harmony**, is sometimes rather jazzy, as in the case of the chord progression below from Bartók's *Sonata for Two Pianos and Percussion*, which includes this passage of triads piled on top of one another.

Stravinsky was also fond of suggesting two chords at once, for example in this very well-known chord from *The Rite of Spring* in which E major and E flat (with a seventh) are combined.

The secret to writing a successful pandiatonic chord progression is to devise a strong tonal chord progression first. Write it out and find ways of 'blurring' it by adding notes not related to the chords. Some pieces make a distinct feature of this effect, for example the orchestral piece by Charles Ives, *The Fourth of July*. This depicts a street celebration in which two bands, each playing different music, converge on a street corner, intermingle chaotically, and then continue on their separate ways.

Devise a progression of chords (about eight chords in all). Each chord should be made up of two other chords, similar to the Bartók and Stravinsky examples above. Now write the chords out with accompaniment figurations for piano and add a melody line for another instrument.

Write a short piece in ternary form. For the opening 'A' section use *only* chords made up of intervals of a perfect fourth. For the middle 'B' section choose another interval to which to restrict yourself.

Choose a composition with simple tonal harmonies. Work with a friend. Each copy out the piece, adding notes to the harmonies so that, as the piece progresses, the chords become increasingly blurred. Compare your final result and discuss how you achieved your blurring effect.

## Clusters

No description of twentieth-century chords would be complete without mentioning clusters. These are blocks of tones and semitones, rarely written out in full with all the accidentals, but indicated only by the top and bottom notes. There are no hard and fast rules for clusters; some composers have written clusters which include microtones as well as semitones (listen to Penderecki's *Threnody to the Victims of Hiroshima*) whilst others have written black-note and white-note clusters for piano, leaving out the semitones.

Clusters can produce vivid effects, as in the example below for piano, but as they are more usually employed as a textural device they are covered in further detail in Chapter 14, along with a composition exercise.

# CHAPTER FOURTEEN

# Techniques and Textures

The last chapter showed different ways of devising scales and sets of pitches. This chapter is about linking those pitches to durations and rhythms to construct simple ideas. There are two main headings: melody and rhythm, and (on page 157) counterpoint and texture.

## Melody and rhythm

Most of the melody writing covered so far in this book has been based either on Classical or pop styles, where rhythms and phrases are nearly always regular and the music is underpinned by a chord structure.

In much twentieth-century music there is no regular rhythm and chord structure; the composer has to invent something to take their place. A range of techniques is discussed below. You should approach them with an open mind and feel free to use or adapt them; they are not sets of rules.

### *Melodic and rhythmic cells*

A cell in music is a small unit which, combined with others, makes up a larger structure. You could, at the start of composing a piece, decide upon a set of cells.

First, invent a set of pitches.

Then invent a rhythm for them.

These cells could be used to construct phrases and counterpoint. The following example features the original cells, some transposed and some inverted.

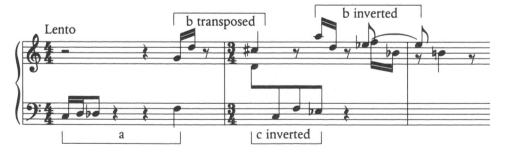

Alternatively you could choose to write the rhythms first and then add pitch.

## Exercises

Compose a melody about sixteen bars long which employs one or two cells. Then add an ostinato accompaniment with pitches and rhythm based on the original cells.

Compose a short two-part piece for instruments. Each part should be based on a different and contrasting cell, so that the two parts are truly independent. The example below shows first the cells on which the two instrumental melodies are based.

Cells are an economical way of composing, but they can be limiting. A piece based solely on a handful of melodic fragments is likely to force you into 'thinking small' and of concentrating on detail at the expense of the overall form.

### Rhythmic series

The last chapter described how to construct a note-row. It is equally possible to construct a row of durations and use this as a **rhythmic series**. This one consists of twelve durations.

First, set out all twelve durations in order, from smallest to largest:

Now put them in an order of your choice to form a series:

Such a series can be varied using some of the techniques available for varying a note row (see Chapter 13). The series could be reversed or rotated using permutations similar to those used in bell ringing.

One of the most obvious ways of combining pitches and note values would be to pair them off, perhaps in the form of a table:

Composing a piece using this table could be done in a very similar manner to the 12-note examples in the last chapter. Just as composing with twelve notes in strict order ensures that there is no feeling of key, so composing with twelve durations will ensure there is no sense of metre.

However, working with a series of twelve different durations may mean that the music you write tends to be neither fast nor slow, but always in between, perhaps boringly so. One solution to this is to construct different series – some using short note values (to produce faster music) and others using longer note values (for more sustained passages).

The German composer Stockhausen devised a number of interesting ways of controlling the rhythm and pace of his compositions. In order to ensure contrast between fast and slow passages he devised a **tempo scale**. This involves deciding on a set of metronome tempi ranging from the slowest to the fastest. This range is then divided into 8 (an 'octave' tempo scale) or twelve (a 'chromatic' tempo scale) and the composition consists of several sections, each in a contrasting tempo (as in *Piano Piece V, Zeitmasse* and *Gruppen*).

## Exercise

Construct a tempo scale. The one in this example is for a piece in six sections. The slowest section will be ♩ = 60 and the fastest will be ♩ = 120.

The difference between the two tempi is 60 and this will have to be divided by five in order to calculate the five new tempi.

Thus $120 - 60 = 60$

$$\frac{60}{5} = 12$$

1st tempo   60

2nd tempo 60 + 12 = 72

3rd tempo 60 + 12 + 12 = 84

4th tempo 60 + 12 + 12 + 12 = 96

5th tempo 60 + 12 + 12 + 12 + 12 = 108

6th tempo 60 + 12 + 12 + 12 + 12 + 12 = 120

These six tempi can then be allocated to the sections of the composition to create variety of pulse. If they are arranged in ascending order the piece will accelerate, and it will slow down if they are placed in descending order. More usually Stockhausen mixes them up for contrast.

In some of his pieces Stockhausen controls speed and texture by deciding how many notes will sound in a particular section. Obviously if a lot of notes are played during a short section the music will sound fast, whilst if fewer notes are played the section will sound slower. In *Zyklus* for percussion, each of the percussion instruments is allowed a certain number of attacks. This allows the composer to control not only how much we hear of each individual instrument but also the thickness of the texture. Try composing a percussion piece in three or four sections using graphic notation. Decide on the total number of times each instrument will play and draw up a plan showing how these attacks are distributed amongst the instruments and sections. The illustration below is a piece for xylophone, drums and cymbals. The xylophones will play 18 attacks, the drums 24 and the cymbals 7.

Tempo: 1 bar = 10 seconds

## Isorythm

This technique was very common in the fourteenth century and has been revived by composers like Harrison Birtwistle and Peter Maxwell Davies. It consists of a series of notes, called the **color** and a series of durations called the **talea**.

Note that there are more notes than durations. This has an important effect when we start to combine the notes with the durations.

Obviously the series of durations runs out first. At this point, the set of durations is repeated from the start, and the remainder of the notes are used. When the series of notes run outs, it too is repeated from the start.

Eventually the beginning of the color and talea will coincide again. Calculating how many repeats of the color will be required for a full cycle of color and talea is not too difficult if you follow this formula:

$$\frac{\text{lowest common multiple of color and talea}}{\text{number in color}}$$

Thus, if the color has six notes and the talea four durations you will need to work out the lowest number into which they both go; this is 12. Now divide 12 by the number of notes in the color. The answer is that there will be two repetitions before the two coincide.

[151]

Isorhythm is a valuable technique because a great deal of variety is possible with very little material.

Using this formula you could devise a set of interlocking phrases and melodies, perhaps a canon or a series of long phrases like the word pieces in Chapter 3.

## Exercise

Devise an isorhythmic chant. Choose a word or phrase (the name of a football team or an advertising slogan). Work out how many syllables there are (e.g. 'Manchester United' has six syllables). This will be your color.

Now clap a rhythm. This will be the talea, and the number of individual notes it contains must be different from those in the color. Now try and fit the words to the rhythm.

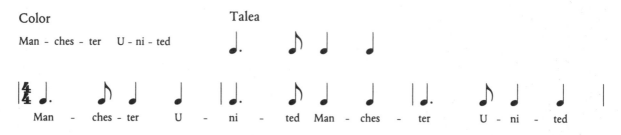

Now try fitting several isorhythmic phrases together in a short piece for two or three performers.

### Using proportions

A simple number series or set of proportions can be employed to create rhythm in a similar way to that in which the rhythmic series was constructed above.

Assume that 1 equals a semiquaver. The series 2 3 5 will produce the following:

This set can be used in any order, producing six possible versions:

When pitches are added a wide range of variations are possible by re-ordering both pitches and note values. You could devise a table with note values on the left and pitches on the right, using the lines and columns to mix and match. The example below consists of the note values above, combined with a group of three notes in different orders. Obviously with only three notes and three note values there will not be much variety in the music. You will certainly need more of both, although the example shows how such a system might be used.

A phrase might be constructed as follows: note values from line A with pitches from line F, followed by note values from line D with pitches from line B.

Some of Bartók's pieces are composed using proportions from the **Fibonacci series**. This is a set of numbers made by adding each new number in the set to the one before.

1   2   3   5   8   13   21   34   55   89

Bartók developed an interest in melodic phrases whose lengths were based on these proportions and not the more common four- and eight-bar structures of Classical music. For example, the first movement of *Music for Strings Percussion and Celesta* is 89 bars long and the climax of the movement ocurrs at bar 55.

## Exercises

Compose a minimalist piece in which the length of the ostinati (or, if you prefer, the number of notes in them or the number of repetitions) are governed by proportions or a number series.

Study Bartók's *Sonata for Two Pianos and Percussion*. Count, in beats and bars, the length of the melodic phrases and the lengths of some of the sections. See if you can find any examples of the Fibonacci series. Try composing a short piece in ternary form based on these proportions.

## Palindromes

Phrases which are the same both forwards and backwards have been popular with contemporary composers because they offer a way of constructing ideas which are perfectly symmetrical.

In the examples below the middle of the palindrome is marked *.

Phrases can be palindromic in pitch:

In rhythm:

Or both:

Palindromes are quite easy to construct but are sometimes hard for the listener to detect. This can be useful, since in a well-crafted composition you may not want too many of your workings to show.

## Exercises

Compose a piece for a melody instrument and percussion. The melody part should consist of two- or four-bar phrases whose pitches are palindromic, while the percussion part should be rhythmically palindromic.

Try composing a **crab canon**. This consists of a melody combined with its own mirror image. Some writers have suggested that such counterpoint is not a canon at all, since it is customary to begin together and since you are unlikely to hear the second part as being related to the first. However, a successful crab canon has a certain curiosity value. This one is based on an octatonic scale:

[154]

As we saw in some of the examples above, your choice of note value is very significant in determining the speed of the music. It is possible to control this speed very tightly.

The rhythm in the example below starts off in steady minims, gradually accelerates to semiquavers, then slows down again. This is achieved quite simply by subtracting a semiquaver in each bar until only semiquavers are left. It slows down again by adding semiquavers.

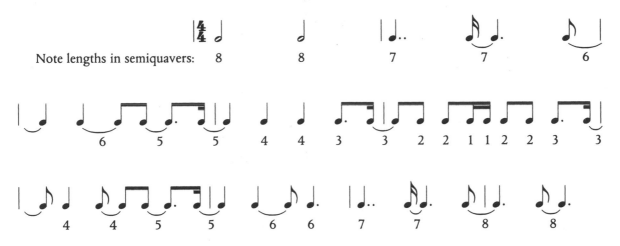

This technique could be employed if you wished to compose counterpoint in which the parts were all moving at different paces.

**Metrical modulation** occurs when a new note value (a fraction of the basic beat) is established as a new beat. In the example below a triplet crotchet becomes the new beat.

Tempo changes using this device are particularly associated with the American composer Elliot Carter. His pieces have a sense of rhythmic unity, since many tempi are derived from the original beat, often arrived at through a process of change similar to the examples above.

## Exercise

The example below shows how a piece can be written using the principle of metrical modulation. It is a **Study** for side drum. A study is a piece intended to strengthen and exercise a particular skill in the player – in this case, counting note-values accurately.

The phrase structure is as follows:

Letter A    Semibreves accelerating to quavers

Letter B    Quavers slowing down to minims

Letter C    Triplet crotchets

Letter D    The triplet crotchet becomes the new beat – i.e. keep on playing at the same speed, but count 4

Letter E    Go back to the start, counting in this new tempo.

Because of the tempo change the performance will get faster each time you repeat. See if you can clap or play it on a table top with a pencil and see how many repeats you can play until the speed forces you to give up. Try writing a similar piece yourself.

---

*Rhythmic freedom*

Not all contemporary music has strictly notated note values. If you have read Parts I and II you will remember that melodies can be represented in graphic form or by using proportional notation.

In some compositions rhythm is not a significant feature, so precise note-values are not needed. This means that the player decides what to do within the guidelines you have given, and brings the idea to life rather like an actor interpreting a line of speech in a play.

For example, most melodies are constructed in such a way that some notes are important whilst others fulfil a only a decorative and supportive role. Less important notes might be articulated in a flurry as a set of grace notes, whilst the ones which require stressing may be long and sonorous. Although rhythm is not strictly notated in the example below, the way it is written gives a clear indication how it should be played and which are the important notes.

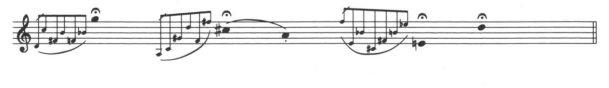

---

## Exercises

Study the instrumental parts in Henze's *El Cimarron*. The notation includes examples of graphic, proportional and staff notation. Try performing some of the simpler sections in which rhythm is not specified. Compare your performance with someone else's.

Compose a long melody with freely notated rhythms. Write one which might be suitable to accompany a slow, solemn procession, or which might form a flashy show-piece for the performer.

## Counterpoint and texture

One of the features of modern counterpoint is that sometimes, few if any of the individual parts are on the beat. This effect can be achieved quite easily by writing out the music as series of block chords and then introducing syncopations.

The following example consists of a set of three-note chords. You could use the techniques discussed in the last chapter to devise the chords themselves.

The middle note is retained on the beat. The outer parts are syncopated with the introduction of ties and rests.

This is not proper counterpoint, although the parts do sound independent. Such a texture might be useful if you wished to break up an otherwise block-like progression of chords.

### *Canons and imitation*

The technique described above is a fairly crude way of composing parts. You may find that canons and imitative counterpoint produce more independent part-writing.

The last chapter included an example of canon using a note-row. Parts can be canonic in several ways.

The pitches are in canon but the rhythm is free:

The rhythms are in canon but the pitches are free:

A **mensuration canon** is one in which the parts move at different speeds. This was a popular device in fifteenth-century vocal music, and has found favour amongst a number of composers in this century, particularly Peter Maxwell Davies.

In the example overleaf the note values in the middle line are twice those in the top line. Those in the bottom line are one-and-a-half times as long as in the top (i.e. a quaver becomes a dotted quaver).

Compose a short choral setting of a psalm for two vocal parts and an instrumental bass. Use modes or scales (see Chapter 13) but avoid writing parts which singers will find awkward. Write the two vocal parts in canon (you can choose whether this is a pitch canon or a rhythmic canon).

Compose a short fanfare for two brass instruments. Try to build it on the principles of a mensural canon.

## Aleatoric counterpoint

This term means counterpoint based upon chance. It can be produced by giving each player a phrase which is repeated over in the form of a free ostinato – so in some respects it is related to minimalism (see Chapter 5).

Usually this type of counterpoint takes the form of a set of ostinati with players entering one by one. No note values are given, and the players set their own tempo within broad guidelines given by the composer (e.g. 'fast' or 'slow'). In the resulting counterpoint there is no precise control over the way the individual parts combine, and this is usually left to chance.

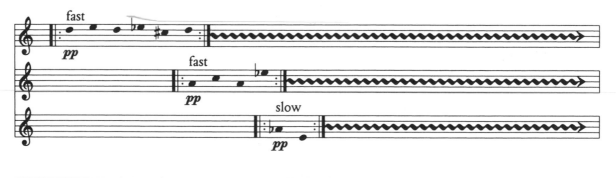

Compose a piece using aleatoric counterpoint in which each of the instruments represents a character in a play. You should devise a structure and story-line in which there is sometimes only one character being heard, sometimes two in conversation and sometimes perhaps the entire cast shouting or arguing.

You can control the texture in several ways:

Spacing    If all the ostinati are in the same register the effect will be like a dense, moving cluster. If, however, they are spaced widely apart they will sound more like independent parts.

Tempo    Although rhythm is often left to the player there is no reason why you cannot be specific and write everything out – the players will then keep their own time independently of each other.

## Monophonic music

Not all new music is as complicated as it sounds. A melody like the one below:

can sound highly complex when spread over the piano keyboard like this:

A **monophonic** texture consists of a single line of music. Many passages which appear to be complex are in fact monophonic in origin. In the following example the same phrase is scored for three instruments in such a way as to retain its monophonic form even though some of the notes are sustained slightly longer than in the original.

This type of texture, which consists of isolated notes (or groups of notes) rather than sustained melodies or counterpoint, is sometimes called **pointillism** after a style of modern painting which featured dots of paint rather than continuous brush strokes. Composers whose music was pointillistic, such as Webern, concentrated on instrumental colour, rather than melodic ideas.

The **Klangfarbenmelodie** (literally, tone-colour melody) was a technique in which the notes of a melody were split up and given to several instruments. The word means 'a melody based on timbres' and the technique often involved wide leaps so as to accommodate instruments in different registers. It is particularly common in the work of Schoenberg and Webern.

### Exercise

Try composing a Klangfarbenmelodie. Write the melody first, then divide it up. Make sure the 'joins' are not too hard for the players.

## Clusters

Cluster chords were introduced in the previous chapter. Although they can used percussively they are equally effective when sustained.

## Exercise using clusters

Compose a piece for two electronic keyboards. In the example below the keyboards are set so as to play a sustained, organ or string-like sound while the player holds down the keys. The clusters are employed to produce blocks of sound which are blended and contrasted.

Each bar lasts 5 seconds, and the clusters should consist of black and white notes. Use the volume control for loudness/softness. Some keyboards are not capable of playing many notes at once — in which case you may need to make adjustments to some large clusters.

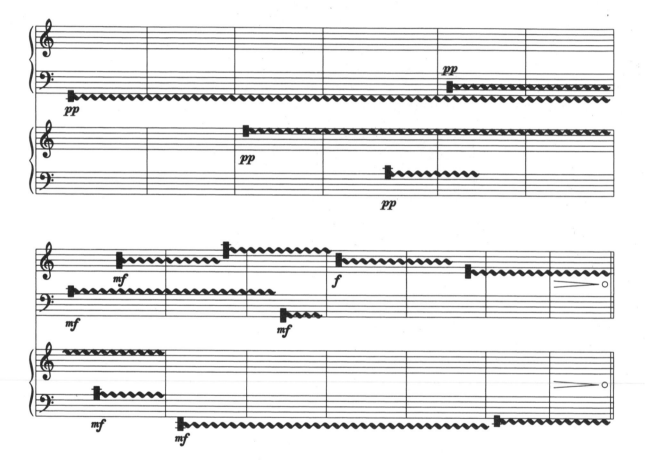

Such a piece does not have to be based on clusters but can involve any chord type, including tonal chords.

When you have written a piece for keyboards, try adding other instruments: a percussion part or sustained strings.

# CHAPTER FIFTEEN

# Form and Process

'Form' refers to the shape of a piece – the number of sections or the order in which certain ideas are repeated. 'Process' refers to the mechanics of the music, the planning of modulations or musical climaxes or perhaps the gradual transformation of a motif.

Composers in this century have developed different ways of exploring the relationship between form and process, as these examples show:

a)  A minimalist piece might consist of a single ostinato which, over the course of time, transforms into a different ostinato. Here the music consists of a continuous process taking place rather than a succession of sections.

b)  By contrast consider this simple graphic composition:

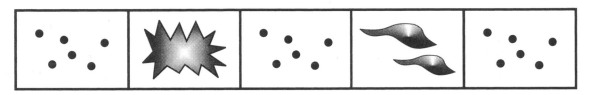

Here the listener will be aware of three sections being the same or similar and two being contrasted. There is no hint in the graphics that one section should lead to another or be related in any way. The sections are like plain building blocks which make up a form but there is no process involved other than simple contrast.

Unlike other chapters in this book dealing with form, this one contains few hard and fast rules. There are no new forms to be learned because this century has been one of experiment and adaptation, with composers tending to explore their own ideas in their own way. Compare, for example, the music of Debussy and Mahler, two composers who were almost the same age (Mahler was two years older) and who both established their careers towards the end of the nineteenth century.

Mahler is best known for his symphonies, which are rooted firmly in the Classical/Romantic tradition. The music is always on the move, modulating and building from one climax to the next. The listener is swept along from introduction to conclusion as the drama unfolds.

On the other hand the music of Debussy seems to drift between different ideas (this, as you have seen in Chapter 13, is partly achieved by using whole-tone scales and chords which do not behave like Classical chord progressions). Many of his forms seem to be based upon contrasting instrumental textures with no obvious attempt to link them together, so the music is often rather static in feel and lacks a developing sonata-type argument.

Debussy's titles provide a clue as to how we should listen: *Nuages* evokes the passage of clouds across the sky; *La Mer* evokes the sea. Listening to the music is like watching a moving scene, and this is one reason why Debussy's style is referred to by a term borrowed from painting – **impressionism**.

Compositions based solely on processes or on visual concepts are examined later. First, here are some examples of traditional forms using modern techniques.

## Traditional forms

There are countless examples of twentieth-century music in ternary form, binary form or sonata form. Indeed, one school of composers (see Neo-classicism, below) has made a feature of forms and styles 'borrowed' from earlier periods.

Clearly, a 'classical' form is easier to construct if the piece has tonal centres and if its rhythmic structure is based on the Classical model of metre and repetition.

The melody in the example below is in binary form. It is based on modes, starting in C, pausing at the double bar on the dominant (G) and returning to C in the second half via a sequence (bars 9–12).

Ternary form has been very popular amongst twentieth-century composers, probably because it has so many ingredients for a simple but effective musical structure; there is an opportunity for contrast in the middle section and the return of the first idea at the end always provides a satisfying sense of conclusion.

## Exercise in ternary form

The piece below is in ternary form and employs a 12-note row.

The first section consists of different versions of the row in canon (the versions are identified in the score, using the system outlined in Chapter 13).

The second section uses the same versions of the row, but in a completely new texture: chords in the left hand, melody in the right.

The third section is an exact repeat of the first (note the *Da Capo* repeat mark), producing a simple ABA form.

Now try an experiment. Play the piece again, but this time don't go back to the beginning to repeat the first section *Da Capo*. Instead, go on to finish with the example below. Whilst this is still canonic and has the same rhythm, it uses a different version of the row so the repeat is not a literal one. Play through or listen to them. How noticeable is the change of notes? Does the change weaken the effect of the repeat or add interesting subtlety?

What conclusions can we as composers draw from these examples? One is that atonal composition allows us much more flexibility with form. In some circumstances an exact repeat is not necessary; the fact that two sections merely sound similar is sometimes sufficient to satisfy the ear that a repeat has occurred. This phenomenon is further explored in the next two sections.

[163]

## Repetition and contrast

Forms based upon repetition and contrast – such as rondo, and the closely related song form (verse, chorus, verse, chorus, etc.) – are employed by many of today's composers.

As we have seen in the last section, repetition does not have to be exact. It is possible to select only certain features of the music for repetition – for example, the same notes with a different rhythm, or repeating the rhythm with different notes.

Repetition of timbre can produce effective results in a variety of ways. If one instrument is featured playing a series of solos the repetition of the solo will tend to stand out, as will passages featuring particular combinations of instruments.

> solo ... all together ... solo ... all together ... (etc.)
>
> woodwind ... strings ... woodwind ... strings ... (etc.)
>
> melody ... percussion ... melody ... percussion ... (etc.)

Passages of alternating texture will often add up to a formal scheme, even if the content of the individual passages is not the same:

> chords ... counterpoint ... chords ... counterpoint ... (etc.)

Clearly the extent to which a listener will be able to relate two passages will depend upon the strength of the connections you make. Nonetheless it is surprising how many alterations can be made to a repeat before the original sense of the music is completely lost. You can try this for yourself.

## Exercises in repetition

Compose a short and simple atonal piece. Now repeat it several times to a small audience. At each repeat change a small detail. Ask the listeners to put their hands up when they think they have lost track of the original. It is usually possible to make quite a few seemingly major alterations before the hands go up.

When you have tried the above exercise, try writing a piece in several sections. Compose the sections in such a way that each has something in common with another. For example two sections might have the same or similar rhythms. Two might be built on identical forms of a note-row. See if your audience can spot the similarities.

Listen to the music of Harrison Birtwistle. An image he is fond of evoking is the *musical landscape*. Imagine a scene in the country; there will be the sky, trees, fields, buildings. The scene will never be the same two days in a row; sometimes it will be raining, in winter there will be no leaves on the trees. Yet the scene will always be recognizable. Birtwistle applies this principle to music. Passages always sound similar, even though there is much variation from one version to the next.

## Form and the visual arts

In their quest for new forms many composers have turned to modern painting, particularly work which features abstract designs and patterns. Examples of this can be seen in the paintings of Mondrian, Matisse, Klee and Miro. Here, form consists of a careful balance between certain colours and shapes. Klee coined the phrase 'asymmetrical balance', suggesting that balance could be achieved between two apparently unrelated ideas.

Compose three completely contrasted musical passages, A, B and C. Now play them through in all six possible orders:

ABC,   ACB,   BAC,   BCA,   CAB,   CBA

The chances are that you will find some combinations more pleasing than others. This is because they achieve a better balance. Try to identify what features create this balance.

Now listen to each section individually. Which one would you most like to hear repeated? What are your reasons? When you have decided rearrange the piece with your chosen section at the beginning and end. For instance, if you preferred the order BCA and, of the three sections, you had decided to repeat A, you would add A to the begining, making the overall structure ABCA.

Listen again. Does the repetition strengthen the piece? Or does it ruin the balance? In deciding, try to avoid long, agonized deliberations; your first instinct is very often the one to stick to.

## Transformations, variations and systems

Some variation techniques are examined in Chapters 6, 7 and 12. These can be employed to change one idea into another – in other words, to **transform** it. For example, a motif could be progressively altered until it became something quite different.

Transformation is a common technique in minimalist composition. This is sometimes called **systems music**, reflecting the fact that pieces unfold according to a system, or process. In the example below an ostinato is transformed by adding notes on the end and subtracting them from the beginning.

For other ways of transforming an ostinato, see Chapter 5 on Minimalism.

Some minimalist pieces are based upon melodic or rhythmic transformations which can take some time to complete and can be very complex.

Transformations should be planned carefully with attention given to the following:

► How many beats or bars does the transformation take?

► Does it take place in stages, or in one continuous process?

► What features of the original are transformed?

These issues, like the design of a note-row, constitute a part of **pre-composition**, the process of planning a piece. The worked examples below should give some idea how much pre-composition might be needed to make a particular process or piece possible.

## Exercise: transforming an ostinato

The example below involves the transformation of a consonant and smooth ostinato into a chromatic and jerky one. It is achieved using a simple alternating two-bar pattern. In the first bar a rest is introduced. In the next bar a note is chromatically altered.

The complete process takes 8 bars to complete.

## Exercise: transforming a note-row

This process employs two techniques at once: isorhythm (see page 151) and permutation (see pages 141–145). First you will need a 12-note row (the color) and a rhythmic series (the talea).

The note-row is 12 notes long and the talea is 5 note-values long. The formula (page 151) tells you that the row will repeat five times before the start of the talea and the start of the row coincide again. The transformation involves altering the row at each repeat by changing the order of the notes.

First the row is divided into groups of three:

In each repetition of the row one of the groups will be altered so that, by the end, the notes of the row are in a different order.

The whole process – that is, the row and its four altered versions – looks like this when written out isorhythmically:

## Indeterminacy and chance

Musical games and compositional processes involving dice were discussed in chapters 3 and 13. One of the reasons that some composers have relied upon chance rather than making decisions for themselves is because music composed using chance is unlikely to include any ideas or influences unconsciously borrowed from other pieces or composers. The odds are very high that the music will be completely original.

In some cases chance is employed to construct a note-row or rhythmic series. Chapter 13 shows how this can be achieved using the numbers on dice, playing cards and dominoes. Composers have also adopted sets of numbers from sources completely unrelated to music, for example, pages of telephone numbers selected at random or numbers taken from scientific tables.

Involving the performers of a piece in the decision-making process is another way of introducing chance into, for example, the pitches used in a melody:

Or choices of phrases:

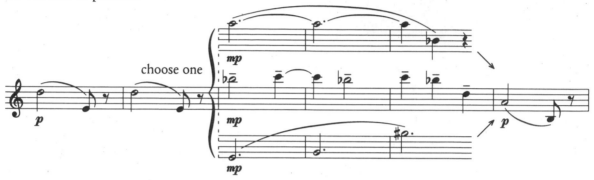

The above examples are mostly concerned with the smaller features of a composition – individual notes and rhythms or melodic phrases. The overall form of the piece can also be determined by chance, perhaps by tossing a coin to decide the order of sections.

In this example the head side of the coin represents an 'A' section and the tails side a 'B' section. If the coin were to be tossed six times you might come up with the following:

heads   heads   tails   heads   tails   tails

Translated into form this might become:

A  A  B  A  B  B

Chance has been adopted by composers who believed strongly that the process of composition should be free of all influences and be based upon random principles rather than forms and ideas handed down by history. John Cage, when working with the dancer Merce Cunningham, used dice to decide not only the content and form of the dance score, but where the dancers moved on stage.

## Tone poems and free forms

Many of the forms described in this book have been expressed like formulae, for example AABA. There are, however, many ways in which music can be constructed without following this 'building block' principle.

One is the **tone poem**. This was particularly popular with late Romantic composers and involves constructing a piece around a story or scene. Usually there needs to be a strong sense of narrative – perhaps a journey. Alternatively you could choose a theme with a very focused mood – the supernatural, perhaps, or space.

## Exercise

Think of (or invent) a short story with a few simple episodes. Write a synopsis of your story in one column and your musical ideas in another. The story in the example below is an imaginary discovery of a lost planet.

| Story | Music |
|---|---|
| Drifting in space | Soft cluster chords |
| Sighting of new planet on radar | Bleeping |
| Set course and accelerate | Ostinati getting faster |
| Slow down, enter atmosphere | Violent, bumpy phrases |
| Land | Silent, mysterious |

Forms blt around textures can be more fluid than those built in sections. For example, a piece employing clusters (see page 146) could be constructed according to the 'thickness' of the textures and the way they expand and contract. The diagram below depicts the overall shape of a section of such a piece. The scale across the top gives an indication of time in seconds.

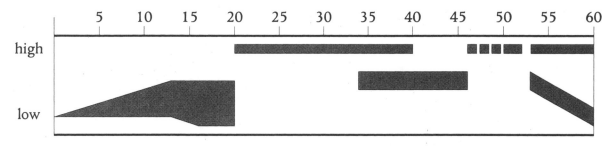

## Quotation and parody

The practice of basing compositions on ideas taken from other composers, periods and styles is not new; in the sixteenth century the technique of **parody** involved composing an original piece using motifs taken from another composition, often a well-known tune. Popular tunes were also quoted by Mozart in the banqueting scene of his opera *Don Giovanni*.

These practices are not to be confused with plagiarism, which involves stealing someone else's ideas and passing them off as your own. In Mozart's case the quote was intentionally a public joke. In the case of parody composition the technique is a legitimate one where the composer is completely honest about using it. Don't forget, though, that today's copyright laws may prevent you from using other people's music in this way unless you get their permission first.

In this century the practice of quotation and parody has taken a number of forms.

### Neo-Classicism

Neo-Classicism arose around 1918 as a reaction to the Romantic style. It is particularly associated with Stravinsky and is characterized by an avoidance of the emotionalism of the nineteenth century and a borrowing of forms and styles from earlier periods (mainly, though not exclusively, the Classical period).

Much has been written about the theory of neo-Classicism. The composing practicalities are fairly straightforward. Textures tend to be traditional: melodies with accompaniments, imitative counterpoint, canons and fugues are common. Forms are based on Baroque and Classical models such as chaconnes, binary and ternary forms and sonatas. Composers do not always stick to the 'rules', however. In a sonata, for example, the development section may be left out.

Most neo-Classical music tends to be tonal, but employing modes and octatonic scales gives it a 'Classical music with wrong notes' feel (this feature is also discussed in Chapter 13).

The following worked example is a dance movement, perhaps for a modern ballet. It employs an octatonic scale (i.e. one with eight different notes).

The form is the same as that of a typical Baroque dance movement – binary. For the purpose of this exercise it will be based on a real one by Bach, the minuet from the French Suite in E flat. There is no need to carry out a thorough analysis. Here we see Bach's minuet with the thematic ideas identified by letters. (Note the first- and second-time bars at the repeats. These mean that when you play a section you play bar 1 first, then repeat. The second time round you play bar 2.)

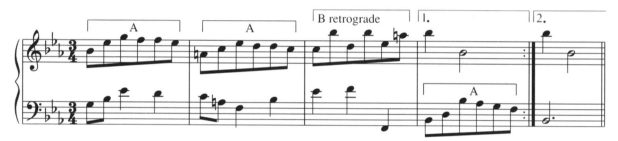

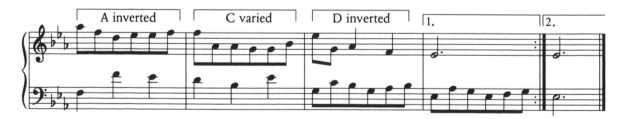

Following this model, a blank score is set out showing the thematic scheme and tonal outline.

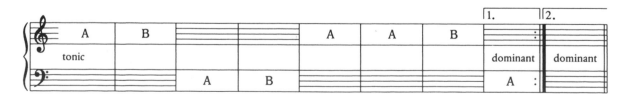

| | C | D | C | D | A inverted | C varied | D inverted | 1. | 2. |
|---|---|---|---|---|---|---|---|---|---|
| | dominant | | | supertonic minor | | | | tonic | tonic |
| | | B | | A | | | | | |

The score is now filled in. The ideas are new, but match the original structure.

Not all pieces are based so closely on an original scheme. In some cases the scheme is extensively adapted or even invented from scratch. The point about the style is that you, the composer, borrow whatever you think you may need to get going.

### Found objects

This is a term borrowed from the visual arts. 'Found objects' are exactly what their name suggests: real-life objects which the artist had found and incorporated into a painting, design or collage.

Some of the simplest examples of found objects in music occur in **musique concrète**, a type of electro-acoustic composition (see overleaf) in which pieces are created using sounds recorded in the 'real world'. One of the most striking pieces of musique concrète is Stockhausen's *Hymnen*. This is based on recordings of national anthems of the world along with background radio noise.

Found objects also appear in some instrumental music and can take the form of musical quotations inserted into a composition. One composer who has employed this device to startling effect is Peter Maxwell Davies. Although his compositional style is basically atonal many of his pieces introduce fragments of tonal music ranging from plainchant to punk rock. His *Eight Songs for a*

*Mad King* depicts George III, who in his later years roamed the passages of Windsor Castle raving and insane. At times the king sang arias from his favourite operas by Handel and attempted to teach the birds to sing. The score contains passages of opera, dance music, tweets and whistles.

Although the technique of quotation can be very theatrical and effective it usually arises because there is a relationship between the main body of the piece and the music being quoted. One idea is very often transformed into another. An instance of this occurs in Berg's Violin Concerto where a Bach chorale is quoted in the last movement. The 12-note row employed by Berg for the concerto is quite closely related to the first few notes of the chorale.

## Exercises

Composing pieces which involve a mixture of styles can often produce comical results. Only you can decide what you want to achieve. It may help if you work exercises which draw upon ideas taken from the pieces above. You should back up your composing with listening.

▶ Write a piece based on the idea of *Hymnen*. This could employ anthems (as Stockhausen does), or perhaps well-known melodies, nursery rhymes, etc.

▶ Write a dramatic piece about time-travelling, including hints at a number of different historical styles.

▶ Write a tribute or an *In memoriam* to a composer whose work you admire. Include quotes from one of his or her compositions in your own.

▶ See if you can take a well-known melody and transform it, in slow stages, into another well-known melody.

## Electro-acoustic composition

Electro-acoustic music is neither a form nor a style, but it is characterized by the use of electronic instruments and equipment. A full study of the techniques and equipment available is outside the scope of this book. This section is intended to show briefly what is possible, and to suggest ideas.

The raw materials of electronic composition are sounds which have either been recorded or created from scratch using electronic instruments. The term *musique concrète* has been used to describe music based on recorded sounds from the real world, but this term is rarely used today; modern technology has made it possible to transform almost any sound into anything else, so it matters little where the original comes from.

### Making your raw materials

There are three main sources of sound: those recorded using a tape recorder, those recorded using a sampler, and synthesized sounds.

Microphone recording can be accomplished with very little equipment: a microphone and a tape recorder (some tape recorders have built-in microphones). It is not necessary to go into a studio to record sounds – the inside of pianos and bathrooms provide resonant acoustics and a large cardboard box or packing case will provide a cheap 'booth' with dead acoustics.

Sampled sounds are very accurate but samplers tend to be quite expensive. These are electronic recorders which memorize a sound and replay it at any pitch when connected to a keyboard. Unlike a tape recorder, which has constantly to be rewound, samplers provide 'instant' replay with additional options: trimming the start and end (so as to get a clean sample), looping (so the sample sustains or repeats), reversing the sample, and mixing it with other samples.

Synthesizers tend to be associated with popular music and are usually used to play their preset sounds, imitating pianos, organs, strings, brass and other instrumental timbres. It is possible to create your own sounds on a synthesizer, or to remodel the preset ones. Although different makes of synthesizer vary there are three very basic operations involved.

The first is to change the **waveform**. Waveform is the word used to describe electrical sound. When a sound is converted into an electrical signal it travels down a wire in vibrating waves. If the vibrations are smooth then the sound will be smooth, like the vibrations from a tuning fork.

Sine wave

If the motion is jerky the sound will be harsh, like a buzz.

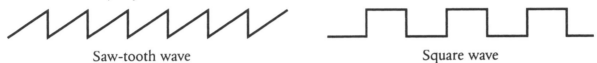

Saw-tooth wave                                     Square wave

The type of waveform determines the tone-quality of the sound. Most modern synthesizers produce their sounds using two or more oscillators (an electrical circuit which produces sound at a particular pitch). Depending upon the way in which these oscillators are tuned and connected together it is possible to determine the type of waveform. The keyboard controls usually allow you to select particular set-ups and to 'tune' the individual oscillators.

The second way of controlling sound is by using **filters**. These are devices to remove parts of the sound and alter its tone-quality. The tone controls on a hi-fi set are simple filters.

The third operation involves altering the structure of the **envelope**. This might be described as the 'shape' of the sound. For example, a note on a piano starts very suddenly as the hammer strikes the key and then dies away slowly. This shape – a sudden start (the attack) and a slow dying away (the decay) – is the envelope.

The envelope described above relates to the loudness or softness of the sound: whether it starts loud and dies away or starts soft and builds up. The correct name for this type of envelope is the **amplitude envelope**.

There are other types of envelope. Adjusting the **pitch envelope** allows you to tune the sound very finely – perhaps it starts with a short glissando as it slides up to its pitch, then drops away at the end to be flat. Many instruments do this naturally, although we tend not to notice. The keyboard may also allow you to adjust the **filter envelope**. This allows you to control the speed and amount by which the filtering starts and dies away.

Sounds – whether they come from an instrument, sampler or tape recorder – can be treated in a wide variety of ways by passing them through a range of effects devices. It is now possible to purchase effects units with a range of options including echo, reverberation and chorus (an effect which artificially thickens a sound). Another device, popular with composers of electro-acoustic music, is the **ring modulator** which transforms the timbre of a sound.

## Compiling the piece

This can be done using a tape recorder or, if you are using samplers and keyboards, a sequencer.

Much electronic music can be compiled using a reel-to-reel tape recorder. Sounds can be slowed down or reversed (by putting the tape in back to front). With two tape recorders sounds can be recorded, one on top of another, to build up thick textures. Tape can be cut and joined together using a splicing block and a razor blade. This technique can be employed to make tape loops, in which a sound is recorded on tape, cut out and then joined end to end. When it is fed back into the recorder it passes round and round so the sound is continuous.

The invention of multi-track tape recorders was a great bonus for the electro-acoustic composer. On a multi-track it is possible to record several tracks at once, like orchestral parts. This is usually done by **overdubbing**, recording one part then rewinding and listening to that part while you record the next on another track.

The sequencer is used rather like a tape recorder but does not record the music. Instead it records the mechanical details of the performance. It only works when connected to an electronic instrument (usually a keyboard) by a MIDI cable. MIDI stands for Musical Instrument Digital Interface, a system for connecting electronic instruments.

To set up a sequencer the player turns it on to 'record' and performs the piece, or a section of it. The sequencer remembers which keys were pressed, along with other performance information (e.g. pedalling), and it is usually possible to build up the performance both in layers, like a multi-track recorder, and in sections. On playback the sequencer operates the keyboard by remote control, reproducing your original performance as if you were playing. It is possible to correct mistakes, copy and re-arrange sections.

There are different types of sequencer. Some are built into a keyboard and some take the form of computer software. These can display the composition on screen as notated music, and some can also print it out.

Some of the best electro-acoustic compositions are those which exploit the possibilities of the equipment and produce music which cannot be produced in any other way. Processes include inventing sounds and shaping timbre, looping sounds, layering, playing backwards, speeding up and slowing down.

In very general terms electro-acoustic compositions fall into three types:

► Pieces involving transformations of sounds and ideas. These could be synthesized or natural sounds, changed and re-shaped by a synthesizer or effects unit.

► Pieces made up of contrasting ideas and textures, like a collage or scrapbook.

► Pieces made up of layers of different materials and textures. This could combine 'live' players with electronics – perhaps a 'backing tape' or the sound of the live instruments amplified and distorted.

# Part V

# Popular Music

Some aspects of popular music have already been covered in this book.

You may find it helpful to review these pages before starting on this section, although it is not absolutely necessary.

Popular music has a number of features which make it quite different from music belonging to the Classical tradition. One is that it is rarely written down. Composers and players tend to work by ear, and although some songs are published as sheet music this usually takes the form of the vocal part with a piano arrangement and bears little relationship to the sounds actually heard on record.

Generally popular music is recorded, either on tape, vinyl or CD, and this has given it a very close relationship with music technology and electronic instruments. This relationship is now so important to the composition of popular music that recording and other production techniques are specially covered in Chapter 18.

# CHAPTER SIXTEEN

# Songs and Styles

The most common form in popular music is the song. Whilst there are many instances of purely instrumental compositions – some of these have even reached the charts – the vast majority of popular music is vocal. If you are intending to compose popular music seriously you will have to learn how to set words to music.

Performance of your songs might cause a problem, since some people feel shy about singing. Here are a few ways round the problem:

▶ Write the song for someone who can sing. This will mean that you have to take the range of their voice into account, and you may have to compose your song in a key which suits the singer.

▶ Write the song for a group of singers. The individuals may not mind performing so long as they are all in it together.

▶ Play the vocal line on an instrument.

▶ Write a choral piece (like gospel) for the whole class, or write a rap where singing is not required.

▶ Take the plunge and have a go at recording the song yourself. There are a number of recording techniques available which will make you sound much better than you (think you) are. These techniques are discussed in Chapter 18.

There are two types of popular song. One is the ballad. This is composed using techniques similar to those of traditional harmony and counterpoint; in other words the song consists of a melody and accompaniment with cadences and clear chord progressions. The accompanying instrument is usually a guitar or keyboard, and the inclusion of other instruments – the arrangement – usually takes place after the song has been composed.

The other type of song is based on a repeated riff or drum pattern, and it is the structure of this ostinato which gives the music its characteristic feel, for example rock 'n' roll, reggae, funk or 'house'. Here composers usually start with the pattern and leave considerations like chords and form until later. What is important in the early stages is getting the feel right.

## Words

Whichever type of song you choose you will need to know how to set words to music. Usually composers start with the words and then devise a melody to fit, although it is possible to work the other way round and write the melody first.

Lyric writing is a skill in itself and it is only possible to touch upon it here. Many lyrics are made by borrowing from or adapting poetry, but be careful not to use anything in copyright because you will have to seek permission if you intend to perform it publicly. Writing your own lyrics (or getting someone to write lyrics for you) is not so hard.

A good lyric needs to be based on a memorable and interesting idea, perhaps by using a catch-phrase or by conjuring a picture in the listener's mind.

## Exercise: brainstorming lyrics

Take a large sheet of paper and start writing phrases and words. A rhyming dictionary and a thesaurus (a dictionary of words of similar meaning) might help. When something catches your eye write it down on a separate sheet and see if you can develop it, for instance like this:

▶ *Dancing in the park*
This could be extended simply by repeating the opening word:
    Dancing, dancing, dancing in the park.

▶ *Fast car*
This could build into a sequence of paired words:
    Fast car, go far, bus stop, must stop, fast lane, back again.

▶ *Lonely sidewalk*
This could be used to start off a series of similar rhyming lines:
    Lonely sidewalk, where am I?
    Lonely sidewalk, touch the sky,
    Lonely sidewalk, free as air,
    Lonely sidewalk, I don't care.

The next chapter shows how to compile a complete song. For the moment you will need just enough words – probably a verse and the chorus – to get started on the melody. Don't forget that in song form the melody is repeated – it's the words which change. So words for extra verses and sections can always be added later once you are happy with the tunes.

Suppose you decide to use the 'Lonely sidewalk' lyric as a chorus. You now need to start a new writing process for a verse. Try to make sure the rhythm and pulse is the same for both verse and chorus. For example, suppose you settled on this rhythmic setting for the chorus:

Then the verse will need to have the same time signature – that is, four beats in a bar. Keep this pulse in your head, and try writing or clapping a rhythm and scribbling down words which you think may fit.

    Al - ways  rain - ing
    Close  the  cur - tains

As soon as you have a collection of phrases you can try arranging them into a rhyme.

    Always raining, always raining, shutting out the sun,
    Close the curtains, slammed the door and got my shoes to run.
    Always raining, always raining, couldn't see the street,
    Help me, help me find some quiet, help me find my feet.

Lyrics do not *have* to rhyme, though they often do and there are a number of standard rhyming patterns, the two most common being:

    A A B B – e.g. sun, run, street, feet.
    A B A B – e.g. sun, street, run, feet.

Lyrics with rhymes tend to have a clear rhythmic structure which can be helpful when you are trying to find a melody to fit. The best way to improve your lyric-writing skills is to study other people's lyrics and poetry, and practise as often as you can.

## The ballad

Assuming you have a set of lyrics, ballad song writing can be approached in a number of ways.

### Starting with the melody

First, decide on a rhythm for the words.

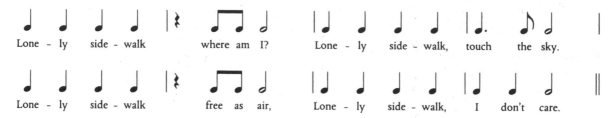

You may get interesting results by placing the strong beat in a different place.

Now, working bar by bar, sing the words on a repeated note gradually introducing intervals and phrases until you hit upon a melody you like.

If you are completely stuck you could start with a repeated note and introduce new notes one at a time.

These techniques, including ways of building the above ideas into a complete melody, are similar to those covered in previous chapters. However, the words add a new dimension; the intervals, whether falling or rising, have a special significance. The two contrasted settings of the words below provide two slightly different meanings to the words.

Falling intervals and sad:

Rising intervals and hopeful:

Having completed your melody, try to work out from the notes what the chords might be. This procedure is explained on page 29.

### Starting with the words

Another way of starting a song is to indicate in the lyric where the chord changes might occur. Write out the words and rhythms and mark possible places for the chords.

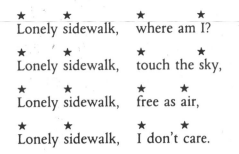

The next stage is deciding on the chords themselves. Techniques for devising a chord progression are covered in Chapters 4 and 17.

To start with, keep things simple. Generally the chords should follow the lyric so that, for example, an eight-bar lyric should be matched with an eight-bar progression. However, you may feel it appropriate to try two chords per bar as in this example:

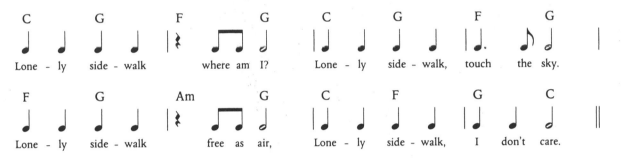

## Composing a hook

Some songwriters prefer to start by composing the most important phrase in the song – the one listeners will remember afterwards and perhaps go away humming. This is the **hook**, and may be as short as two notes. The important thing is that it is memorable.

Hooks are usually placed in the chorus, though not always. In the case of 'Lonely sidewalk' this phrase could become the hook, and would need an interesting setting.

Alternatively the second half of the line could be the hook, taking the form of an answering phrase.

Working with hooks takes a little experience, since it is easy to get stuck after an initial good idea. One way round this is to go on to compose a completely different part of the song – perhaps the verse. This may feed you with new ideas, or may provide you with a natural lead in to the hook you have just composed.

## Adding a backing

Once you have worked out the melody and chords you will need to decide on the figurations to be adopted by the accompanying instrument. The examples below are for keyboard, but the principles could equally be applied to guitar.

Two very common figurations are block chords and arpeggios.

The backing could be even simpler than this – perhaps a repeated riff.

There are ideas for creating a fuller arrangement in Chapter 18.

## The riff-based song

Anyone who has used a drum machine or the auto-chord function on a keyboard will be familiar with the selections of repeating one- and two-bar rhythmic patterns identified by style-name: 'rock', 'reggae', 'electro' and so on. Every style has its own individual rhythm (and the tempo is usually a crucial factor). This is supported by the other instruments, which contribute to the overall feel of the music.

Getting the feel right is the key to many pop music styles. Most are based on a combination of rhythms and riffs which together form an ostinato pattern. Like drum patterns the typical ostinato is only one or two bars long and can be repeated throughout the entire song or varied slightly from verse to verse.

The examples below, along with the analytical notes, show some typical patterns and riffs in a range of styles. These are intended to convey the general characteristics of the style and should certainly not be considered as rulebook copies.

### Rock 'n' roll

Much rock 'n' roll is based on chords I, IV and V (e.g. C, F and G). Four-bar chord progressions are very common, also the twelve-bar blues.

First, the 'classic' rock 'n' roll bass line with drums. Note the dotted rhythms in the second half of the bar. The bass riff repeats, transposed up and down according to the chord.

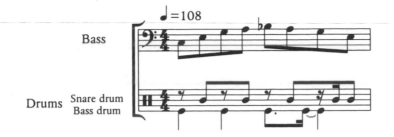

Rock 'n' roll often features a characteristic piano figuration developed by Fats Domino and Jerry Lee Lewis (note the similarity with Ska and Reggae).

The guitar pattern below, with percussion, is in the style of Bo Diddley. This particular ostinato often continues unchanged throughout the song.

Ideas for listening: Eddie Cochran, Gene Vincent, Bill Haley, Buddy Holly, Jerry Lee Lewis, Fats Domino, Bo Diddley.

### Rhythm and blues

Rhythm and Blues (or 'R & B') is the forerunner of modern rock. It began when country blues singers, who were used to accompanying themselves on solo guitar, moved into the cities and began to sing with bands involving piano, bass and drums.

The most common pattern consists of a strong, pounding pulse with a triplet feel. The off-beat is stressed very strongly by the snare drum: this is the 'back-beat' typical of rock. For this style the twelve-bar blues form is very common.

Ideas for listening: B B King, Chuck Berry, early Rolling Stones and Eric Clapton.

## 'Rock' or 'heavy rock'

'Heavy rock' was originally used as a term in the 1970s to distinguish it from rock 'n' roll and R & B. Many features of heavy rock are present in the music of today, although they tend to come under the more general term 'rock'.

One of the main features is the use of heavily amplified guitars; in fact the style is dominated by the guitar, whose sound is usually treated with some kind of distortion. This is achieved by playing through a pedal-controlled distortion device (see page 212); the sound is generally harsh and sustained, producing characteristic 'power chords'.

Chapter 5 shows how rock chords are based on the pentatonic scale. Chords drawn from the 'flat' side of the key are common (for instance in the key of E major these are D, A, C and G). Rock musicians play chords with a characteristic form of syncopation, and this is a key to the style. Chords tend to be played (or 'pushed') just ahead of the beat. Because of this syncopation the drums tend to be simple, providing stablity with a strong and very loud stress on the off-beat.

Related to this is the chordal guitar riff: a loud, percussive and syncopated sequence of chords. In this example the hi-hat plays crotchets, leaving the guitar quavers exposed in the texture:

Ideas for listening: Jimi Hendrix, Led Zeppelin, Queen, Z Z Top, Bruce Springsteen.

## Heavy metal

The main difference between rock and heavy metal is that the playing in heavy metal is more aggressive and virtuoso.

In much heavy metal the guitars and bass guitar play fast pentatonic riffs in unison.

In the drums there are twice the number of back-beats, giving the impression of great speed.

Ideas for listening: Iron Maiden, Metallica, Van Halen, Def Leppard.

[182]

## Electro rock

This was popular in the early 1980s, and made a special feature of keyboard synthesizers and drum machines. Consequently it tends to have a rather clockwork feel. The texture was usually a three-part one: a simple rock drum part, a keyboard bass line (with characteristic left hand octaves) and a keyboard countermelody with very little syncopation. The minor mode was common.

Ideas for listening: Ultravox, Human League, Jean Michel Jarre, Pet Shop Boys (more recent but heavily influenced).

## Reggae

Reggae is usually played more slowly than rock, and is characterized by the chords being played on the off-beats while the drums stress the third beat. The bass should be prominent, and often employs repeated notes.

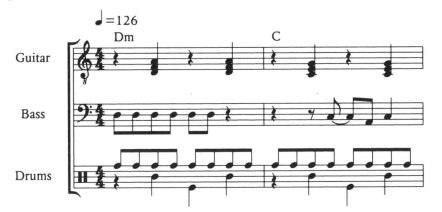

The pattern tends to continue hypnotically thoughout the song. Even the chords form part of the ostinato, being a two-bar sequence. The most common are tonic–supertonic (e.g. C to D minor), tonic to flat leading note (e.g. D minor to C) and tonic–dominant (e.g. D minor to A minor).

There is also a common version of the reggae rhythm in compound time:

Ideas for listening: Bob Marley, Aswad, Burning Spear, Maxi Priest.

## Ska

Ska (along with its close relatives bluebeat and rock steady) is fast reggae. There are four off-beat chords per bar in a triplet rhythm, giving it a breathless feel. It is related to some rock 'n' roll piano patterns (see above).

Ideas for listening: Prince Buster, Desmond Dekker.

## Soca

Reggae and ska is the music of Jamaica. *Soca* (short for soul-calypso) originates in calypso and steel band music which comes from Trinidad. The steel band is a melting pot of styles and cultures and these are reflected in soca. The most characteristic feature is the bass line with its Latin rhythm (see page 24) and off-the-beat chords, not unlike reggae. The drums employ a fast semiquaver hi-hat beat which has been borrowed by disco.

[184]

It is also common to add Latin-American percussion. Chapter 18 shows how to build up samba-type textures. Soca can also involve extended instrumental solos.

## Funk

Funk is a mixture of styles: blues, rock, jazz and Latin-American. According to the jazz player and writer Graham Collier the word means 'dirty', and was adopted by jazz musicians who regard the style as 'impure'. Its most characteristic features are its catchy, syncopated rhythms and jazzy chords. The example below is made up of the following parts:

Keyboard/guitar:    This part could be played by either instrument. It consists of syncopated chordal stabs. The chords themselves are sevenths on the tonic and supertonic. These and similar jazz chords are explained in the next chapter.

Bass:    This is a melodically simple ostinato with dotted rhythms. In funk, many notes are played either just before a beat or just after. The player often plucks the strings or taps them with a thumb to produce a pecussive sound.

Drums:    The basic beat is rock, but with a fast semiquaver pattern on the hi-hat. Note the 'lifts', notated by a cross note-head.

This two-bar pattern can be repeated over and over. Ideally the performance should settle down into a comfortable 'groove' in which all the players find their rhythmic place. In funk there is a tendency towards longer instrumental solos than would normally be found in a pop song, and the style has tended to attract jazz players.

Ideas for listening: Spyro Gyra, Al Jarreau, Mat Bianco, Roy Ayers, Simply Red. Many of Michael Jackson's songs have a strong funk feel.

## Soul

Soul music is a hard style to pin down because it draws on so many sources. Written down it looks very similar to rock, so it may be helpful to start with a summary of the principal differences between the two.

One of the main differences lies in the way the vocals are performed: rock is blues-based and tends to be sung by white artists; soul is gospel-based and tends to be sung by black artists. Soul requires quite a mature singing voice and artists tend to be older than in rock.

Soul tends to feature chords drawn either from the diatonic scale or from jazz. 'Rock-type' chord sequences featuring the flat side of the key are rare.

Rock is a guitar-based style whereas soul makes more use of keyboards, backing instruments (brass and saxophones) and backing vocals. Soul often features quite elaborate orchestral arrangements with a large string section.

Like rock, soul falls into a number of categories and these are closely linked to its historical development.

▶ 'Atlantic Soul' is so called because it was associated with artists on the Atlantic record label during the 1960s – Aretha Franklin, Wilson Pickett, Sam Cooke, Otis Redding. The style was related to gospel and often employed chordal patterns based on chords I, IV and V, which were originally intended to support a congregation, but which night club singers were quick to exploit for their hypnotic singalong potential.

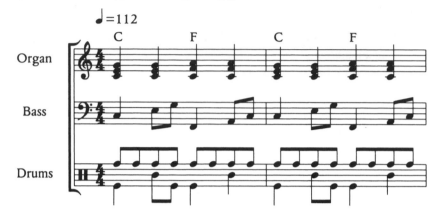

▶ Tamla Motown – named after the 'motor town' city of Detroit where many of the artists (e.g. the Miracles, the Supremes, the Four Tops, Marvin Gaye, Stevie Wonder) came from and where the record company was based. In comparison with Atlantic the style was light and dance-like, featuring riffs with skipping rhythms. The drum parts tended to avoid a strong back-beat, although this was sometimes provided by a tambourine.

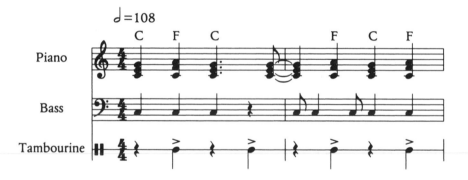

*Rap and Club Dance*

These styles are extremely difficult to reproduce without access to the appropriate technology, and a fuller description of them appears in Chapter 18. However, the basics can be covered here.

Most raps are performed to a pattern of drums, percussion, electronic sounds and bass. Many of the drum patterns are drawn from rock and funk, and they are usually played by a machine.

Dance music, such as house, techno and hardcore is much faster. The bass drum is often no more than a repeated crotchet and is used to accompany a variet of heavily syncopated riffs and sound effects.

[186]

The drum patterns and many of the riffs include electronically repeated notes which could only really be played by a machine.

Ideas for listening:  Dance – Basement Jaxx, The Prodigy, Chemical Brothers
Rap – Eminem, Public Enemy, Ice T

## Word setting and riffs

Setting words to music in the above styles involves a slightly different technique to the one discussed under ballads.

Vocal melodies based on riffs tend to be chant-like rather than melodic. They often revolve around one note and are pentatonic, as in this rock vocal part:

### Exercise: writing a song over a riff

First write your words. Then, keeping in mind what style the song will be in, try reciting them in different rhythms. You might accompany yourself by playing your backing riff on guitar, bass or keyboards, or you could use a drum machine or just tap your feet.

You can employ the techniques for composing riffs discussed in Chapter 3.

When you are happy with your rhythm sing the phrase through quietly on a repeated note which you can reach without straining. When your 'performance' is secure start to vary the notes until you have a melody you like.

You will probably find that unlike ballad writing you do not need to plan the chords at an early stage – this is because riffs often last for several bars before there is a chord change.

## Exercise: writing a rap

Word setting for a rap obviously calls for a different approach. You could try the brainstorming technique described on page 177.

The words consist of short, punchy phrases, like graffiti. They are recited in time with the backing. Rhymes are quite common, although unlike song lyrics the lines are not always the same length, nor do they have the same rhythms.

> Don't try
> To satisfy
> The crowds are pushing
> I can't get by
> To find a solution

These words might be performed as follows – although the end result will be much freer than the written-out example suggests.

The best way to learn to rap is to listen to other rappers. Pay special attention to the word accents and breathing spaces. Sometimes the words will be divided between two rappers (a leader and chorus effect).

## Improvising

It may seem odd to include improvisation in a book about composing but it plays such an important role in popular music that it deserves a mention.

Improvisation is a common way for pop musicians to generate ideas, and the following exercises should help you to develop your improvising skills. They are based on a call-response idea which was introduced in Chapter 2 (see page 10).

For most of the exercises you will need some kind of backing. This could be provided live (handclapping will do), or by a drum machine, auto-chord or even a karaoke tape.

Always try to improvise as a group – or, at the very least, in pairs. If you are not a very confident improviser there is nothing worse than having to wait your turn for a solo.

## Exercises

Devise a backing. This could be a simple riff or drum pattern, and it will need to include a bar's rest.

While this pattern is repeating improvise something to go in the bar's rest. You can make the rest longer or shorter, depending how much you want to improvise.

Start with something simple. Try improvising a handclapped pattern. Then try playing a repeated note in an interesting rhythm. Once you are secure with that, add another note to your repeated-note phrase, then add another.

Now try something more difficult – improvising around a chord progression. Start with a simple two-chord pattern (like reggae or simple funk) and play a riff, transposing it up and down according to the chords.

Now try improvising something for one of the chords.

Then improvise a little more. Then try this with a four-chord progression.

You may find it helpful to record your improvisation sessions. Not only will this help you keep track of your progress, it will also save any interesting ideas which may come up.

# CHAPTER SEVENTEEN

# Chords and Structures

A great deal of popular music can be written using only basic triads, but your songs can be made much more interesting if you widen your knowledge of different chord types.

First, a quick reminder of Chapter 4, where chords were introduced.

The most commonly used and simplest chords are called triads because they contain three notes. Each of the three notes has a name: the bottom note is known as the **root**, the middle note the **third** (because it is three notes up) and the top note the **fifth** (because it is five notes up).

It is possible to extend this chord by adding more notes above the fifth.

In the chord above, where C is the root, the extra notes are named thus:

B is the **seventh**
D is the **ninth**
F is the **eleventh**
A is the **thirteenth**

Like triads, chords containing these additional notes can be built on each degree of the scale.

Chords do not have to be played using the arrangement of notes given above. In particular, the note with the highest number (7th, 9th, etc.) does not have to be at the top. The use of different voicings will make the chords not only easier to play but also more effective. Voicings are explained in Chapter 5.

If you play guitar you might try experimenting with the voicing of the chord by altering your fingers on the frets. You may find this easier if you look at a chord manual and learn some **inversions**. This is the term often used by guitarists to describe alternative ways of playing chord shapes (although the term has a slightly different meaning in Classical harmony).

On a keyboard you would usually play all four notes of the seventh chord but it is not necessary to play all the notes of ninth, eleventh or thirteenth chords (in any case, it is unlikely that all the notes will fit under your hand, either on the guitar or the piano). Instead you can hint at the chord by playing selected notes.

There are no rules to determine which notes you should play and which you should leave out. Your ear is the best judge but always try to include the root, the third and/or fifth, and the note which is numbered in the chord symbol.

## Types of sevenths

This section is about the structure and naming of different types of seventh chords, and the following section on dominant chords covers some examples of ninths, elevenths and thirteenths. However, the harmony of popular music rarely gets more complex than this, so for a full description of ninth, eleventh and thirteenth chords a book on jazz harmony is recommended. In some cases it is possible to create interesting effects without very much theoretical knowledge. These are described later in this chapter (see *pedals*, *sus chords* and *added chords*).

There are different types of sevenths depending upon the component intervals. Here are the scales of C major and C minor with their various sevenths identified by chord symbols:

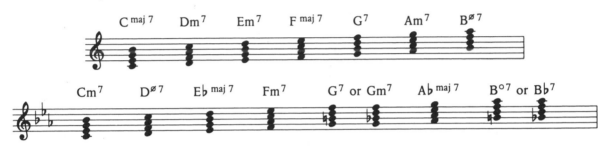

In these scales there are five different types of seventh:

### Seventh

This is a major triad with a minor (or 'flat' or 'flattened') seventh (sometimes called a 'dominant seventh', which is incorrect unless the chord actually is rooted on the dominant).

### Major seventh

This is a major triad with a major seventh.

### Minor seventh

This is a minor triad with a minor seventh.

### Half-diminished seventh

This is a diminished chord with a minor seventh.

### Diminished seventh

This is a diminished chord with a diminished seventh.

## Dominant chords

The dominant seventh was introduced in Chapter 10. The dominant seventh in C is G⁷, a chord which can be used in place of plain G at a cadence.

There are many versions of the dominant chord. Get into the habit of experimenting with them. The chords below may look very complicated but the figures are more easily understandable if you think of them in relation to the root. In this way chord symbols work rather like a figured bass.

## Using sevenths and chromatic dominants

Sevenths and chromatic dominants tend to be more common in soul, funk and reggae than in rock and are used to provide extra colour. In most cases the more colourful chord is simply used in place of a normal triad, and the rules of Classical harmony (about preparing dissonances and avoiding consecutives) do not apply in popular music.

In the twelve-bar blues it is customary to add sevenths:

The last four bars have the function of preparing the dominant chord for a new verse and a repeat of the twelve bar. This group of chords is termed the **turnaround**. Turnarounds can be adapted so as to be quite jazzy and do not have to follow the G,F,C,G pattern exactly.

In reggae the characteristic alternating triads on the off-beat can be made more interesting.

A much-used chord sequence such as the one below can be given a new lease of life.

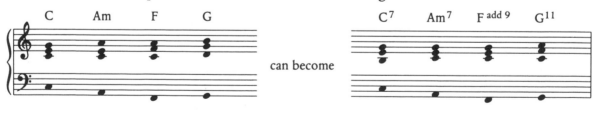

can become

## Exercises

Write out a chord chart (see page 73) for a twelve-bar blues. Choose a key which you do not find too difficult. Then try the following:

▶ different versions of the dominant chord in the last bar
▶ different turnarounds in the last four bars

[192]

- ► altering the chords in some other bars so they form different types of 7th
- ► adding 9ths, 11ths and 13ths to chords

Choose a well-known song, write its chords out and find ways of 'jazzing' them up by adding notes to the existing chords.

Try working out and playing through the chords of a jazz 'standard' – a well-known song, popularly used by jazz players for improvisation. Examples include *Misty, Deep Purple, Don't Get Around Much Any More, Stardust, Take the A Train*. Try transposing them into different keys.

## Melodic dissonance

Sevenths, and other dissonant intervals, can be incorporated into the melodic line in the form of a riff, as in the example below:

### *The flattened fifth*

The **blue notes** are usually the flattened third and seventh. There is another, often used by blues and soul singers, the flattened fifth. It is usually introduced into a minor scale, and its presence is very characteristic.

## Exercises

Compose a two-bar riff which includes dissonant notes. First of all, experiment with the flattened fifth and the seventh.

Then try writing a riff over a bass in which the riff consists entirely of dissonant notes.

## Substitution chords

This is a jazz term and refers to the way in which certain chords are interchangeable. Take for example C and Am⁷. Both chords have the notes C, E and G in common, so that Am⁷ can often be used as a substitute for C.

Thus the chord progression C–F–C–G could become C–F–Am⁷–G.

can become

In the same progression Dm⁷ could also be substituted for F (because both have F, A, and C in common).

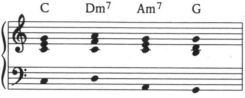

## Pedals

A pedal is a bass line or note which stays the same whilst the chords change. There is no necessity to work out symbols for them. It is usually sufficient to identify the pedal and the chord seperately. Thus, in the example below, the chords are as follows:

C
G/C       (chord of G with C in the bass)
B♭/C    (chord of B♭ with C in the bass)
F/C      (chord of F with C in the bass)

This device can produce some extremely complex harmonies. In the following examples the chord progression occurs over a tonic pedal.

In some songs the pedal effect is achieved differently. In the examples below the bass changes under a repeated chordal riff. The chord symbols describe the underlying chord progression.

[194]

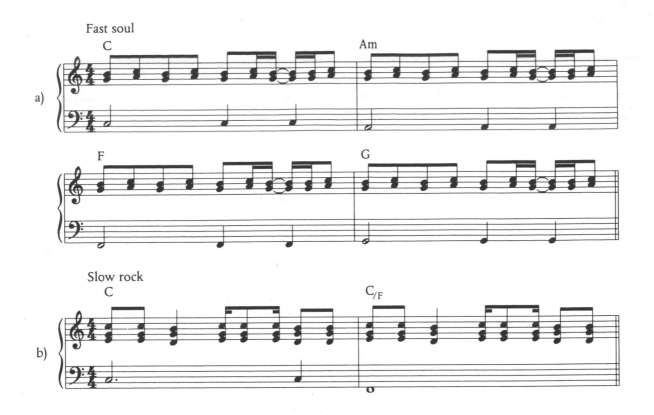

## Suspended and added chords

The most common suspended chord is the 'sus 4' chord. This means that, in a triad, the third is missed out and the fourth above the root put in its place.

The sus 4 chord can be extremely useful since it implies a harmony without being either major or minor. This might give you great freedom in a solo, or allow you to jump between unrelated chords and keys.

'Sus' is short for suspension, this being the pop equivalent of a Classical device (see page 89). The chord contains a 'foreign' dissonant note which replaces one of the notes that is supposed to be there – in this case the third. According to Classical rules the foreign note should resolve onto the missing one but in pop and jazz this may not happen. In fact successions of unresolved sus chords are quite common and may include sevenths for added interest:

### Added chords

The most common added chord is the added sixth, shown below in both its major and minor forms:

Sometimes you will see the chord symbol 'add 9'. This is a direction to add the ninth but not to make up a true ninth chord by adding the seventh as well. In the case of C$^{\text{add 9}}$ this would simply mean adding a D to the chord.

Some very effective chordal patterns and riffs can be made by alternating suspensions and additions.

Riffs like these are quite easy to work out and play on the keyboard, although when written out as a set of chord symbols they look quite forbidding:

C$^{\text{sus 4}}$    C    C$^{\text{sus 4}}$    C$^{\text{add 9}}$    C

They are thus best devised by improvising and experimenting, rather than through arithmetic.

## Exercises

Select some chord progressions from the examples given in Chapter 4 (see pages 32–36) and try the following:

- ▶ play them over a tonic pedal
- ▶ replace some chords with substitutions
- ▶ add 6ths to some chords, and suspend notes in others

Listen to 'In the air tonight' from the Phil Collins album *Face Value* and 'Love comes quickly' from the Pet Shop Boys album *Please*. Both songs employ pedals. Compose a four-bar chord progression over a tonic pedal. Choose a minor key and try to capture the sad feel of these songs. Now compose a simple riff to go with the chords.

## Advanced chord progressions

The chord progressions covered in Chapter 4 involved chords drawn from the diatonic scale or, in the case of some rock progressions, from the pentatonic scale. This is not the place to get into a lengthy theoretical argument about whether a particular chord is pentatonic or chromatic in origin. The purpose of this section in the book is simply to introduce chord progressions not covered earlier.

A chromatically descending bass line is almost as common in popular music as it is in Classical music. It can produce some effective sequences for slow rock-type ballads.

The chords it produces are not chromatic in themselves – the progression is merely a series of inversions of chords drawn from the minor scale. A truly chromatic chord involves introducing notes which are not part of the diatonic scale. One common device is to alter the third of a chord, so that a chord which you might expect to be minor becomes major. Similarly major chords can be altered into minor ones.

| C | Dm | F | G | would become | C | <u>D</u> | F | G |
| C | Am | Dm | G | would become | C | <u>A</u> | Dm | G |
| C | Am | F | G | would become | C | Am | <u>Fm</u> | G |

Chord progressions involving chords with roots a third apart are common in rock.

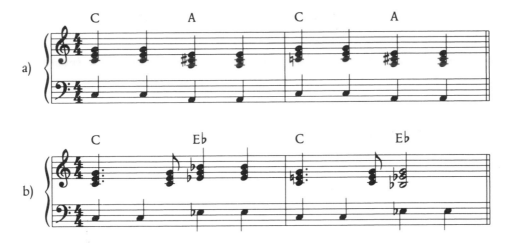

Pairs like these might combine to form a four-bar progression.

Alternating the tonic chord with one either a tone lower or a semitone higher can create a feeling of drive in the music, especially if it is driven by a strong and vigorous riff.

## Four-bar progressions

Phrases can be built around contrasting chord progressions. A four-bar diatonic chord progression can be answered by a four-bar chromatic one.

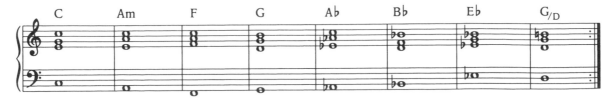

In the above example, the last chord is an inversion of G. The symbol is G/D indicating that D is the bass note. A root position chord would have been possible here, but the inversion makes a smoother progression when you repeat it from the beginning.

Here is another example.

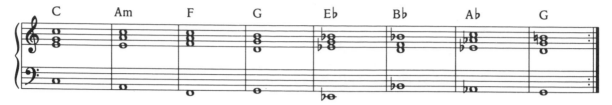

There is a relationship between these 'flat' harmonies and the tonic.

▶ A♭ major is used as a sort of flat relative to C minor. It can be used as a substitute for the tonic.

▶ E♭ is a flat relative to G, and can be used as a substitute for the dominant.

▶ D♭ is the flat relative to F, and can be used as a substitute for the subdominant.

In any major key there are thus three sets of I, IV and V chords:

|  | I | IV | V |
|---|---|---|---|
| tonic major | C | F | G |
| relative minor | Am | D | Em |
| 'relative flat key' | A♭ | D♭ | E♭ |

It is possible to jump quite effortlessly between all three:

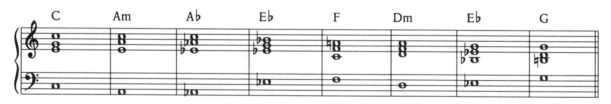

## Exercises

See how many ways you can find of harmonizing the note C. An example is given below in the form of a seven-bar chord progression. Note that C is always at the top.

Study Elton John's song 'Harmony' (included on the album *Goodbye Yellow Brick Road*). In the coda the word 'harmony' is set to a repeated phrase using a succession of many different chords. Also look at the jazz standard *One Note Samba* whose melody is a repeated note with changing chords beneath.

Compose the chords for a short song in AABA song form. Try several versions of the B section in remote but related keys according to the table above.

## Chord progressions not starting on the tonic

It is quite common for rock 'n' roll and soul songs to begin not on the tonic chord but on the subdominant. Usually this involves a short introductory phrase stressing the dominant so the listener expects a tonic chord. Instead the music moves straight to the subdominant and delays the tonic for several bars.

In some of the more jazzy styles of soul the progression may not state the tonic at all, even though, as in the example below, it is strongly implied. Here the last two chords lead the ear towards a C major chord but this expectation is never resolved; the progression repeats again from the beginning.

## Modulating chord progressions

In addition to jumping into remote keys as in the examples above, it is possible to modulate more gently into closely related keys.

The principle of modulation is introduced in Chapter 10, which you should read now. The examples below consist of eight-bar progressions with the modulation in the middle followed by a return to the original key. The progressions either end with a perfect cadence or a half-close.

You will see that the new key is arrived at via its own dominant. The modulation thus requires a V–I progression (or, better still, a II–V–I progression) in the new key. These crucial harmonies are identified in the examples.

In popular music the most common keys to pass through when in a major key are the relative minor, the subdominant and the mediant. In the minor the most common keys are the relative major, the submediant and the subdominant.

**Modulation to the relative minor** (found on the sixth degree of the scale – e.g. when in C major this will be A minor)

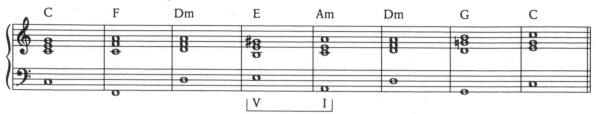

**Modulation to the relative major** (found on the third degree of a minor scale – e.g. when in A minor this will be C major)

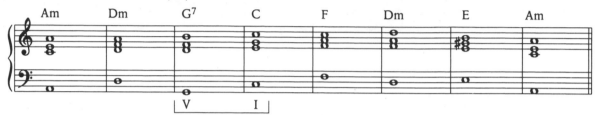

**Modulation to the subdominant** (found on the fourth degree of the scale – modulations here are common in popular music but rare in a Classical style. In C the subdominant will be F)

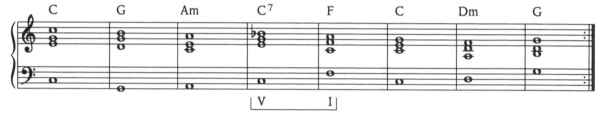

**Modulation to the mediant** (found on the third degree of the *major* scale. This example does not apply to the minor since the third degree of the minor is the relative major, described above. This example is in C, so a modulation to the mediant will take you to E minor)

**Modulation to the submediant** (in a minor key this can serve as an 'alternative relative major' – e.g. in A minor this will be F)

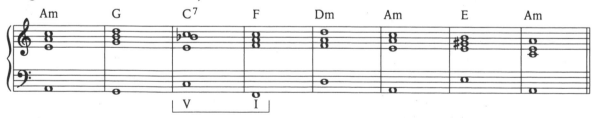

---

## Exercises

Write out a chord chart for a twelve-bar blues but leave the last four bars blank. Now complete these four bars with a chord progression which modulates and prepares the way for a middle section. Try several versions: one which modulates to the subdominant, one to the relative minor, and so on.

When you have done the exercise above, write middle sections to go with the modulations. Don't forget that these middle sections should lead the song back to the home key again.

## Advanced song form

The popular song is made up of a number of component sections; *verses* and *middles* were discussed in Chapter 7.

Being able to compile all these sections requires an understanding of what the terms mean and how the sections contribute towards the overall plan.

| | |
|---|---|
| Verse | A verse is a section which is repeated with different words set to the same tune. It is not usually the most interesting section musically but the words often set the scene or topic of the song, or fill in the details of the story (if there is one). |
| Chorus | The chorus is usually the most memorable section and often contains the title words of the song. It is a good idea to limit the number of choruses, otherwise there is a danger of it losing its impact. |
| Middle | The middle usually involves a contrasting arrangement of instruments and a contrasting key. Sometimes the words involve a slight change of subject. |
| Bridge | The distinction between a bridge and a middle is often hard to make. Usually a bridge serves to link sections together, perhaps a four- or eight-bar modulation leading to a middle, or a mini introduction building to a chorus. |
| Introduction | Not all songs have an introduction. It can be extremely short and simple: a few strummed chords on the guitar or one or two bars of drum pattern. It is also common to play one of the main melodies or backing riffs, perhaps from the chorus. |
| Coda | Many songs simply repeat the chorus at the end and fade out on record with no clearly defined ending. A coda is one way of bringing your song to a halt. Often this consists of a repeated riff or pair of chords, usually something from the chorus so the song finishes on a memorable note. |
| Instrumental | Many songs include an improvised solo, usually based on the chords of either the verse or the chorus. It is rare for this to last more than one chorus or verse. |

### A worked example of a song

This example uses the 'Fast car' lyrics from Chapter 16. Its purpose is to demonstrate how a song might be assembled. The smaller details of how to invent melody and find chords will be left out, since these techniques have already been covered in the previous chapter.

First, the verse:

> Fast car, go far
> Fast car, in the rain
> Fast car, fast lane
> Fast car, back again

This is set to a simple alternating pair of chords with a rock feel. The melody is extremely simple.

Following the form of most songs it is usual to repeat the verse. A new set of words will be needed (in fact you may find you need more verses as work progresses). Try to make sure they fit the melody of verse 1 without having to make too many alterations to the rhythm.

> Fast car, lights bright
> Fast car, motorway
> Fast car, hold tight
> Fast car, Saturday

Now for the chorus. A more interesting melody will be necessary. However, the lyric can be more repetitive since it is desirable for it to stick in the mind. Also, you could take your title from a line in the chorus. This song could be called *Fast Track*.

> Fast track, drive back, see you tonight,
> Fast track, drive back, see you tonight,
> Fast track, drive back, see you tonight,
> Driving on the motorway,
> Driving to your door.

To contrast with the key of the verse (E minor) the chorus will be in C. This is the submediant which can act as an 'alternative relative major' (see page 200). It is quite common to modulate to the submediant in popular music.

Think about varying the harmonic rhythm. In this example there are two chords per bar, compared with one per bar in the verse.

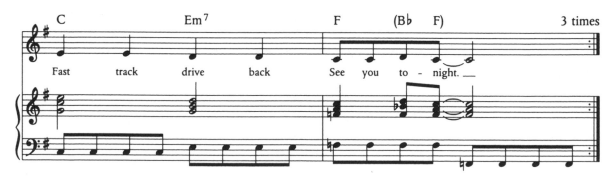

At this stage it would be advisable to play through the verses and chorus to hear how they fit together. In fact, the 'join' is not as tidy as it should be, partly because of the jump to a new key, so a bridge will be added.

The purpose of this bridge is to lead the listener convincingly from E minor to C. It will therefore have to begin with chords related to E minor and end with the dominant of C. Bridges are best sketched out starting with the chords, then adding lyrics and melody.

The chords chosen here are Am, G, F and G. A minor is the dominant of E minor and G is the dominant of C (the key of the chorus).

Here are the lyrics for the bridge:

> Wanna see you
> Wanna touch you
> Can you hear me?
>
> Wanna see you
> Wanna touch you
> Can you touch me?

The three-line structure is deceptive because most of the phrases so far have been four lines long. However, the last word of each line is extended over an extra bar.

The complete bridge is as follows:

The first part of the song can now be assembled and played through:

Verse 1, Verse 2, Bridge, Chorus

These four sections could then be repeated (but you may need to write words for the additional verses). At this point you are half way through the song, and normally the second chorus would be followed by a contrasting section. This could be an instrumental verse, or a middle involving completely new material.

The middle should involve contrast. One way of achieving this is to vary the instrumentation, particularly by thinning it out. Another is to vary the harmony.

Here, the chords are placed over an A pedal, A being the subdominant of the key of the song (if you have read your chapters on chords and form you will remember that the subdominant is one of the commonest harmonies to begin a middle section). Here is the middle with new words. It leads straight into a verse marked 'guitar solo' to indicate that the lead guitarist will improvise a solo.

All that remains before assembling the final version of the song is to compose an introduction and a coda. You will probably need to play the whole thing through a few times to get a feel for what is needed. The complete song is written out on pages 206–207 as a vocal and piano arrangement. There is a simple introduction, two bars of bass. The coda consists of the main phrase of the chorus, repeated.

The overall form is as follows (note the refinements, introduced at this later stage when it is appropriate to 'polish up' the song).

Introduction
Verse 1                     note tonic pedal
Verse 2                     note repeat marks at end of verse (no need to copy out the verse again)
Bridge                      ignore the 𝄋 sign for now
Chorus                      note repeat marks (ignore the 'To Coda' direction for now)
Middle
Verse (instrumental)        note the D.S. (*dal segno*) repeat mark (you repeat from the bridge where
                            the 𝄋 sign appears, saving you the labour of writing out the
                            repeated sections of the song)
Bridge
Chorus (repeated)           after the repeat follow the 'To Coda' direction (this is an instruction to
                            skip the sections the last time round and go directly to the 𝄌 sign).
Coda

---

### More Ideas

Analyse songs. Pay particular attention to the 'joins' – the links between the various sections and the modulations. Also, see if you can write down the order of the sections while you are listening, e.g. verse, verse, chorus, middle, etc.

# Fast Track

Driv-ing on the mo-tor-way, Ar - ri-ving at your door.

**MIDDLE**

Think of you

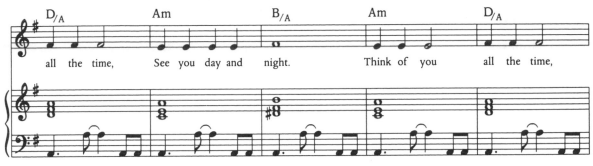

all the time, See you day and night. Think of you all the time,

**INSTRUMENTAL**

Dri-ving through the night. guitar solo

3 times

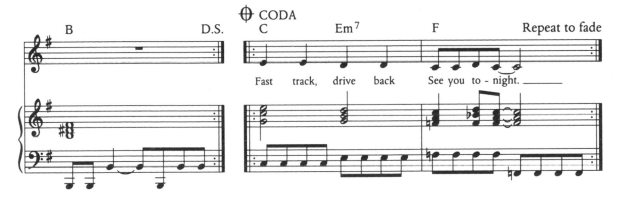

CODA

Fast track, drive back See you to - night. _____

# CHAPTER EIGHTEEN

# Arranging and Recording

Some songwriters work out their song using a guitar or piano before deciding on backing instruments and arrangements. Others prefer to build up the song using multitrack tape recorders or sequencers (the operating principle of these is described in Chapter 15).

Whichever method you choose it is customary to build your arrrangement by working with the instruments in a particular order:

> Drums
> Percussion
> Bass
> Rhythm parts   (in the section below these include guitars and keyboards, tuned percussion, steel pans and Indian instruments)
> Instrumental fills and overlays
> Backing vocals
> Brass and string arrangements
> Instrumental solos
> Lead vocals

## Drums

Most drum patterns consist of three basic parts: bass drum, snare drum and cymbal. The cymbal most frequently used is the 'hi-hat', a pair of cymbals on a stand with a foot-pedal to strike them together. It is usually played 'dry' with the cymbals tightly closed. Sometimes certain beats are stressed with a 'lift': the foot is raised off the pedal to separate the cymbals and create a quick splash of sound.

Typically drum patterns are one or two bars long, repeated over and over. The rhythms in each part vary, depending on the style of the music (see pages 180–187). Drum patterns can be played by a live performer or by using a drum machine or computer. The basic pattern is usually worked out starting with bass drum and snare, since it is nearly always these two which determine the style. Then the hi-hat is added, usually in quavers (known as 'eights' by drummers) but sometimes semiquavers (known as 'sixteens').

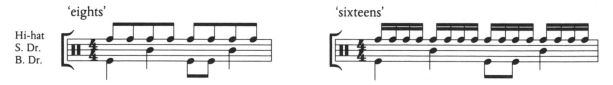

Few drum patterns are maintained all the way through a song without variation. The pattern is often embellished every four or eight bars by a **fill**. In a fill the pattern is broken and a short, decorative solo is played on the snare or tom-toms. Fills provide what drummers call **punctuation** – they help to underline the structure of the song. The current trend is towards simple fills every four bars.

Longer fills, lasting a whole bar, tend to be more common in rock, although they are frequently employed in other styles at special moments – for example to prepare the listener for a coming chorus. Sometimes the fill extends to a cymbal crash to mark the start of the new phrase or section.

It is also standard practice to change the pattern slightly between different sections of a song – for example, verse and chorus. The alteration could take several forms:

- ▶ varying the bass drum rhythm
- ▶ varying the snare drum rhythm
- ▶ varying the hi-hat (in rock and jazz the hi-hat sometimes alternates with the **ride cymbal**, a heavy-duty suspended cymbal with a hard, ringing tone)
- ▶ introducing additional percussion instruments (see below)

Certain parts of the drum sound may be electronically treated; this is usually done at the recording stage. The most common doubling is the snare drum, which is either recorded twice or given a short echo so it sounds 'fatter'. In a lot of dance music it is also doubled by a handclap ('electronic' handclaps are available as a sound effect on most drum machines). Not all songs employ the full kit. Sometimes a solo backbeat can be highly effective, provided by finger snaps, shakers or cow bells (as in the Ben E King classic song *Stand by Me*).

Having worked out all your patterns and fills you will need to compile your drum track, either by working through it with the drummer or by entering it into the memory of the drum machine. This is normally then recorded onto tape.

## Exercise

Drumming seems impossibly complicated to a non-drummer. It may help if you practise playing and writing drum patterns.

▶ Listen to songs and drum machine patterns and see if you can identify and play individual parts – snare, bass drum, cymbals, etc.

▶ Practise playing patterns with your right and left hands on a table top: left hand for bass drum, right hand for snare. Then try playing the cymbals with your right hand instead.

## Extra percussion

The use of extra percussion to decorate the drum track is a matter of style and taste. The most commonly used instruments are Latin American, and these are used extensively in dance music. (Tuned percussion instruments, such as xylophones, marimbas and steel drums are covered under 'rhythm tracks', below).

To do justice to the full range of Latin instruments and rhythms would require a separate book. The following list includes the more common instruments, many of which are included on drum machines.

| Drums | congas (these come in pairs of African-sounding tenor drums) |
|---|---|
| | bongos (also in pairs, but higher pitched) |
| | timbales (pairs of steel-rimmed drums with a metallic ring) |

Shakers        maracas (pairs of seed pods containing seeds)
                           cabasa (a wood and metal cylinder lined with beads)
                           chocolo (a cylinder containing seeds)

Bells           agogo (a pair of conical African bells)
                           cow bell (comes in various sizes from treble to bass)

Miscellaneous   claves and wood blocks (produce a resonant 'click')
                           guiro (a hollow scraper)
                           vibraslap (looks like a baby's rattle on the end of a spring)

Many dance percussion tracks are based on Latin American rhythms such as the **samba**. The tempo is fast and energetic, e.g. 120 beats per minute. First a furious 'backing' is provided by shakers and bells.

This is underpinned by congas in the bass and the claves playing their characteristic syncopated rhythm, known as 'clave'.

Lastly, other parts can be added. Most Latin American patterns are one or two bars long, and it is essential to accent the syncopations.

## Exercise

Work with a group of friends and start with a simple rhythm. Practise playing (or clapping) different accents.

Then try some Latin patterns. You could copy these off a record or a drum machine. Aim at something short, snappy and syncopated. Try building up a texture of rhythms with a group of friends – you may find it helps if you play to a backing provided by live drums or a drum machine.

## The bass

The bass part is one of the most important in popular music – it plays a strong rhythmic role as well as being the driving force of the harmony.

The bass part must always be composed with a sympathetic ear to the bass drum. If, for example, the drummer is 'pushing' the first beat slightly (playing it early) the effect will be ruined if the bass is on the beat or late. It is always a good idea to listen, if you can, to the bass and bass drum together so you can check for any 'bumps'.

Some bass parts consist of little more than the root of the chord played on the first beat of the bar. This can be decorated in a number of ways, either by adding rhythmic interest or by adding passing notes (see also *walking bass* on page 44):

Often the bass part takes the form of a riff whose structure plays a significant role in determining the style of the music (see pages 180–187). Here are some simple ways of turning a single root note into a riff (the example is in C):

---

### Exercises

Working with a friend, choose a song. While one of you plays the backing chords the other should work out a bass part. You can do this together at the keyboard, or with any combination of instruments.

Try this as a quiz. Work out the bass line to a couple of songs. See if a group of friends can recognize the song from its bass alone.

Take a chord progression (from Chapter 4, for example) and compose a set of different bass lines.

---

## Rhythm parts

The rhythm parts provide chordal backing and are usually played by guitar and/or keyboards.

Although acoustic guitars (including the rich-sounding twelve-string guitar) are often used, the electric guitar is the commonest. The guitar sound is almost always electronically treated by using a range of foot pedals. Different styles of pop are characterized by certain effects:

Distortion      used especially in rock and heavy metal. There are various types, ranging in their power from the compressor (fairly subtle) to 'overdrive' (quite a 'dirty' sound and used in punk rock and grunge).

Delay      a short echo, common in rock 'n' roll

Chorus      artificially thickens the sound: a bright, swirling effect often used for slow ballads

The guitar is also used in modern dance music. Here it tends not to strum straight chords but to trigger, electronically, keyboard sounds, using a device called a gate (this technique is extensively used by The Shamen and Asian Dub Foundation.)

The typical keyboard synthesizer has a range of preset sounds, ranging from piano and strings to percussion, orchestral instruments and electronic effects. It is now possible to purchase additional sounds whose electronic data is recorded onto a small card which can be inserted into the keyboard.

Most keyboards also have a facility to alter the sounds in a variety of ways (some of these are described in Chapter 15) and most are equipped with MIDI sockets at the back for connection to other electronic instruments and computers.

When composing rhythm parts for guitar or keyboards it is unusual to specify the number of notes in the chord or to write out the part in detail. The most a player might expect is a clue to the voicing (which note of the chord is at the top) and the rhythm or strumming pattern (if a guitar) in which it is to be played.

Try to avoid rhythm instruments playing throughout the song and, as with drums, try to vary the rhythms. A good arrangement is one where the composer has thought about texture and variety. Keyboard players may need to be reminded not to be too heavy with their left hand, as this might create a second and over-prominent bass part to conflict with the bass guitar.

Don't forget that there are subtle ways of suggesting harmony other than by block chords. Riffs and arpeggios based on the notes of the chord can be very effective.

### Tuned percussion

Rhythm tracks can also include tuned percussion and other featured instruments.

The xylophone and marimba (a 'tenor' xylophone) can either be added using school instruments or using a synthesiser.

Glockenspiels and celestas are invaluable in arrangements of Christmas music but, because of their percussive sound, can also add 'bite' to a chordal arrangement by doubling the keyboard or guitar.

## Steel pans

Steel drums (either real pans or synthesizer sounds) are frequently used in reggae and soca arrangements, either as a melody part:

… or as a backing (note the samba-type rhythm):

The steel band texture is really a four-part one, which can be imitated – up to a point – using xylophones or keyboards. The main parts are:

*Ping-pongs*   the treble, melody-playing instruments
*Guitars*        alto harmony instruments
*Cellos*         tenor harmony instruments
*Booms*         bass instruments

Each player holds two beaters, so the inner parts tend always to be divided as two-note chords. The melody is frequently played *tremolando* (a rapid 'trill' on a single note which is characteristic of steel band music but difficult to imitate on a keyboard).

## Sloop John B

*Indian instruments*

Sitars, harmoniums and tablas are regularly used in bhangra and **ragga** (a cross between bhangra and reggae).

Sitars normally provide counter-melodies and instrumental fills. The harmonium provides chordal support. Because of the way the harmonium is played (not using the little finger) the following scale tends to be favoured because of the arrangement of black and white notes, and this lends a modal feel to any melodies it plays.

In Indian popular music the part played by the tabla is much simpler than in the classical style, and may have drum kit sounds added, especially the hi-hat cymbal. Sometimes, as in European pop, the drum sounds are electronic. The rhythmic patterns themselves are different from standard rock patterns but should aim to have a strong sense of pulse.

## Exercises

Choose a song and write out a chord chart (see page 73) for a keyboard player or guitarist. Find a way of communicating the voicing and rhythm of the part.

Choose a popular song and make an arrangement for steel pans (keyboards and/or percussion will do).

## Instrumental fills and overlays

An instrumental fill is similar to a drum fill and is sometimes employed to tie together two vocal phrases.

An overlay is an instrumental solo combined with a vocal part (usually the instrument is a lead guitar or saxophone).

[214]

You have to decide which of the two parts is more important. Usually an overlay takes the form of a counter-melody to go with the vocal, but care must be taken to balance this both in live and recorded performance.

## Backing vocals

Some of the simplest backing vocals are added electronically. A **harmoniser** is a device which will copy the vocal part and transpose it so that singers can duet with themselves. The most common intervals are a third higher, a sixth lower or an octave lower.

Most live backing vocals are provided by a small group of three or four singers. The technique is derived from gospel, where a dialogue is established between the soloist and the congregation.

In rock 'n' roll the use of nonsense words has become a cliché.

Working out backing vocals can be quite tricky. Not only do you need to know what notes make up a chord, but also which of these will best suit the individual singer's vocal range. In practice these matters are often sorted out by the singers themselves using trial and error. Your ear will tell you if it sounds right. As a rule of thumb avoid high notes as this will make the voices sound too 'operatic,' although in some cases the backing vocals can take the place of instruments supplying the harmony.

## Exercise

Try building up a many-voiced vocal texture over this bass line (which can be played or sung):

## Brass and strings

Full orchestral arrangements are rare in pop, but many arrangements feature brass or strings. These sounds are readily available on synthesizers although live instruments (if available) will add a new dimension. One problem with string chords played on the keyboard is that the sound produced is a piano-type chord, limited by the size of the player's hands. A real string chord can extend over five octaves and include notes right across the keyboard range.

### Arranging a string chord

It is not necessary to study orchestration to write a simple arrangement for strings (although you could usefully read the section on instruments in Chapter 5). The following table shows how to arrange a chord.

| | |
|---|---|
| Violins | These are normally divided into two groups, firsts and seconds. Give them notes above middle C. |
| Violas | Give these notes around middle C. |
| Cellos | Give these bass notes. |
| Double Basses | These normally play one octave below the cellos. |

[216]

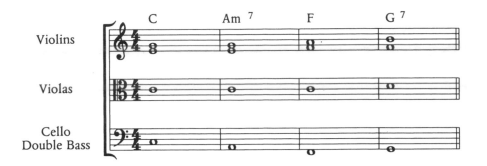

Strings can also play riffs very effectively. In the example below they play in octaves. The best way to organize this is to write out the riff for the players, or play it through to them, and let them decide which octave is best. If you don't like it you can ask them to change.

## Brass

Brass sounds are regularly used by keyboard players in dance and funk styles. However, a real brass section in the band will add tremendous weight to the backing. A typical brass section will include one or more of the following: trumpet, saxophone (of which alto and tenor are the most common) and trombone.

(Note: the saxophone is, of course, a reed instrument, but is usually counted as part of the brass when arranging small wind groups in popular music.)

Brass can be used to replace keyboards and guitars by providing backing chords and instrumental fills. If you do not feel confident writing out the parts or if you are not too sure about the instrumental ranges you can still come up with a passable arrangement by working out your chordal riffs at the keyboard and then allocating the notes in the manner suggested for string chords.

| Trumpet | Notes in the treble (not too high!) |
| Alto sax | Notes in the treble, below the trumpet |
| Tenor sax | Notes below middle C |
| Trombone | Bass notes |

Try to keep the top parts close together – this will help to produce a strong sound.

Don't forget that the trumpets and saxophones are transposing instruments:

Trumpet parts are written a tone higher

Alto sax parts are written a major sixth higher

Tenor sax parts are written a major ninth higher (an octave plus a tone)

The example below is *not* transposed.

[217]

## Recording

There are two principal ways of recording your song: live, and by overdubbing.

### Live recording

This will involve getting everyone together and rehearsing thoroughly, since you will need to record the whole song in one take.

The simplest way to do this is to erect a pair of microphones (two are needed for a stereo recording), connect them to the recorder, press the record button and play. Don't forget to allow a few seconds for everyone to settle down before starting, otherwise you will get all the fidgeting and shuffling on tape as well as the music.

Another way to record live is 'close-miking'. This means providing every singer and acoustic instrument with an individual microphone. These microphones are connected to a **mixing desk** which allows you to balance the sounds. Electronic instruments are usually plugged straight into the desk (but guitars and basses may need first to be plugged into a **DI box** to match the range of their electrical signals to the level required by the desk).

The performers listen to themselves on headphones (this is called **foldback**). The mixing desk is then used to balance the various parts. It sends a stereo signal to a tape recorder.

As an alternative the desk could be connected to a multi-track tape recorder. This will give you the option of recording instruments on different tracks. The making of the master tape (see 'mastering' below) could be left until later.

### Overdubbing

This requires a multi-track recorder. The parts are built up track by track, starting with the drums. When these have been recorded they are played back to the bass player, who plays along with them and records the bass part on another track. This process continues until all the parts have been recorded.

Normally the parts are recorded 'dry' – that is, without adding any echo or effects or changing the original sound in any way. This is carried out at a later stage (as explained below).

Obviously the extent to which you can carry on adding new tracks will be limited by the capacity of your tape recorder. Thus on a four-track you can only record four parts. You can, however, employ two techniques to maximize the use of your equipment.

One technique is called 'bouncing' (some engineers call it 'ping-pong recording'). When a number of tracks have been recorded these are mixed together and recorded onto a spare empty track. The original tracks are now free for you to record over with more parts.

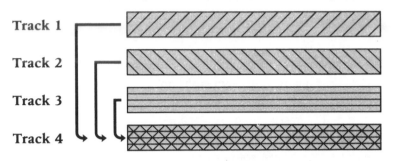

The other technique is to use a sequencer to build up tracks using electronic instruments. Sequencers are explained in Chapter 15. Many parts could be compiled on the sequencer, and some sequencers will allow you to mix them as well. Once you are satisfied with the mix you can then record all these sequenced parts onto a tape track, thus saving space.

## Mastering

This process is also called **mixing down**. It is done at the stage where all the parts have been recorded on multi-track and the object is to mix them all together and record them on a stereo recorder so you have a master tape which can be played on normal equipment.

Mastering involves four basic processes:

### Balance

The volume of the individual tracks is adjusted so each of the parts is heard at a different level. Normally the vocals and drums are the loudest, although the range of possibilities is endless.

### Equalizing

The equalizers on a mixing desk are tone controls intended to 'sharpen up' the tone of the instrument and replace those features of its sound that were lost in the recording process. Many people, however, use equalizers to exaggerate the instruments, making the bass louder and 'bassier' and the cymbals 'hissier'.

### Panning

The pan control allows you to place the sound in the stereo mix so it comes out of the left or right hand speaker. It is thus possible to arrive at a mix in which, for example, the singer is in the middle, the drums are to the left and the bass is to the right.

### Effects

Effects are usually added to enhance the sound in some way. The most common are **reverberation** (which gives a fluid, singing-in-the-bath effect) and **delay** (which is an artificial echo). These are often added to vocals, drums and guitar. They can work wonders for a not very good singing voice.

Another effect is **chorusing**. Here the sound is thickened to give the impression of two instruments. It is used on guitars and cymbals. A related effect, **flanging**, is often used on the bass and gives the sound 'bounce', making it sharper in the mix.

## Technology-based styles

Not surprisingly, the amount of technology available to pop musicians has given rise to some styles of music which are based on – and in some cases dependent on – studio techniques.

### Dub reggae

Dub reggae arose through the practice of trying out different versions of backing tracks. The mixing desk becomes an instrument in its own right; instrumental versions are derived from the mix by turning vocal tracks down, and sometimes altered using echo units so that the piece is completely re-orchestrated. The technique is sometimes featured in live performance, where one or two players will be silent for several bars. A very dramatic effect is often achieved by everyone dropping out to leave the bass playing solo but very loud.

### Exercise

First record some reggae on a multi-track recorder. If you have a four-track recorder you should record drums, bass, guitar and either keyboards or a melody part on the four tracks.

A simple dub version can be constructed using a track sheet as a guide. Bar numbers are across the top. Sections of tracks identified with a cross are played and therefore turned up in the mix. Tracks not marked are silent.

|  | 1–8 | 9–12 | 13–16 | 17–18 | 19–22 | 23–26 |
|---|---|---|---|---|---|---|
| Guitar | ✗ |  |  |  | ✗ | ✗ |
| Keyboard | ✗ |  |  |  | ✗ | ✗ |
| Bass | ✗ | ✗ | ✗ | ✗ |  | ✗ |
| Drums | ✗ |  | hi-hat only ✗ | full kit ✗ |  | ✗ |

Dub has grown into the now widespread practice of remixing. This is especially common in dance and club music where a hit single will be re-released in the form of a new mix, possibly with new parts added.

### Rapping tracks

Many rapping tracks are constructed using the principle of dub. A complex drum and bass pattern consisting of many parts is built up. Each section of the rap is based on different combinations of parts: the **break** consists of a fast 'dub' passage and the **chorus** usually features everything playing.

Here are some examples of parts written out:

The way in which these combine can be plotted on a table.

| Instrument | Break 1 | Break 2 | Chorus |
|---|---|---|---|
| Keyboard | | | ✗ |
| Bass | ✗ | ✗ | ✗ |
| African Bell | | ✗ | ✗ |
| Hi Hat | | | ✗ |
| Snare Drum | | ✗ | ✗ |
| Bass Drum | ✗ | | ✗ |

*Club Dance*

Modern dance music is also based on the principles of dub, but adds another feature: the computer. The parts are recorded and compiled using a sequencer, usually a computer sequencer (see Chapter 15).

Some types of club music, particularly **techno** and **ambient**, employ sound effects or samples – snatches of speech, quotes from pop songs, street sounds and electronic noises. However, rather than running to the huge cost of a sampler, it should be possible to compile your own effects from a keyboard. Pick some out on a synthesizer, or programme in your own (see page 173).

To start with, you will need to record all your drum and percussion parts along with the bass lines and riffs. It is common to add a **sub-bass**, an extra bass part which goes below the bass riff.

Written out the various parts might look like this:

Note that most parts are one or two bars long. Each part is recorded onto a separate track of the sequencer and looped (that is, the computer repeats the two-bar phrases on each track over and over). In this way a continuous texture is built up.

The diagram below shows how the computer will display the tracks. It usually takes the form of a list where you can type in the instrument names against each track. On the left is another column. You can use the mouse (the computer's hand control which glides around the table top) to enter a dot in this column next to one of the tracks, and this will have the effect of silencing the track (a process called **muting**). You can use the mutes to cut tracks in and out.

| Mute | Track | Instrument |
|:---:|:---:|:---:|
| | Track 1 | Keyboard 1 |
| | Track 2 | Keyboard 2 |
| | Track 3 | Bass |
| ● | Track 4 | Sub Bass |
| ● | Track 5 | Tambourine |
| | Track 6 | Hi Hat |
| | Track 7 | Snare Drum |
| | Track 8 | Bass Drum |

Start with all tracks muted. Connect the keyboard/sound-sources to a tape recorder and press the record button. Set the computer running and then un-mute the tracks you want to record (in the manner of dub reggae). A lot of composers, working in the studio, decide the actual order of mutes as they go along, but you may find it helpful to write out a table like the one used for the rap track above, and use it as a reminder.

| Track | Bar numbers 1–4 | 5–8 | 9–12 | 13–16 | 17–20 | 21–24 | 25–28 | 29–32 | 33–36 |
|---|---|---|---|---|---|---|---|---|---|
| Keyboard 1 | ✗ | ✗ | ✗ | ✗ | | | ✗ | | |
| Keyboard 2 | | | | | | | | | ✗ |
| Bass | | ✗ | ✗ | ✗ | ✗ | | | ✗ | |
| Sub Bass | | | ✗ | ✗ | ✗ | | | ✗ | ✗ |
| Tambourine | | | ✗ | ✗ | ✗ | | | ✗ | ✗ |
| Hi Hat | | | | | ✗ | ✗ | ✗ | ✗ | ✗ |
| Snare Drum | | | | | | | | ✗ | ✗ |
| Bass Drum | | | | | | | | ✗ | ✗ |

Some computers are able to remember your sequence of mutes and carry out the operation automatically.

Many examples of club music are much more complex than this. It is common, for example, to have more than one hi-hat pattern, and more than one bass part. This means that you have to record all three versions at the preparation stage. You achieve this by recording the first one, muting it, then recording the second, muting that, and finally the third. You now have three different patterns and can use the mutes to choose which one you want to hear.

Computers vary tremendously in their operation and capabilities. What you compose will be determined by your own skills, as well as by the features available on your equipment.

# Last Words

Whether you have worked through the book to arrive here at the end, or have just opened it at this page, here are a few last words.

Anyone who can pick up a pencil can draw. Anyone who can sing or play an instrument can compose.

Composing is like any other skill. If you want to get better at it you have to practise.

**Listen** to as much music as you can. Analyse it. Find out how it is put together and how it works.

**Play** your pieces. Compose for real people playing real instruments.

**Experiment** with sound. Don't be afraid of making mistakes.

**Have fun** with music. Some rules have to be learnt in order to pass exams, but the most important rules are the ones you make (and break) yourself.

# Index